6-16-76

The Challenge of Urban Economic Development

Goals, Possibilities, and Policies for Improving the Economic Structure of Cities

Michael E. Conroy
The University of Texas at
Austin

Lexington Books
D. C. Heath and Company
Lexington, Massachusetts
Toronto   London

Library of Congress Cataloging in Publication Data

Conroy, Michael E.
    The challenge of urban economic development.

    Bibliography: p.
    Includes index.
    1. Urban economics.   2. Cities and towns—Growth.   I. Title.
HT321.C65   330.9'173'2   75-806
ISBN 0-669-99473-1

Published simultaneously in Canada

Printed in the United States of America

International Standard Book Number: 0-669-99473-1

Library of Congress Catalog Card Number: 75-806

Contents

iv

Preface

This is a book that attempts to translate, synthesize, and condense a selection of potentially policy-relevant technical studies reflecting the state of the art of urban economic development, so that they will be useful to those whose immediate concerns are urban development policies. It is drawn from a substantially longer report by the author to the National Science Foundation, Division of Research Applied to National Needs (NSF-RANN), entitled, *The Challenge of Urban Economic Development: An Evaluation of Policy-related Research on Alternative Goals for the Economic Structure of Cities.* That study was one of four completed simultaneously by the staff of the Center for Economic Development at the University of Texas at Austin in 1974. In the first of the other three, entitled, *The Basic Economics of Metropolitan Growth and Development Goals: An Evaluation of Policy-related Research,* Niles M. Hansen has surveyed, evaluated, and synthesized research on the economics of urban size, urban population growth, goals for urban growth, national urban growth policies, and related areas. The essence of that report has appeared as another Lexington Books publication entitled, *The Challenge of Urban Growth.* The two remaining studies were *A Survey of the Literature on Decentralization of Urban Employment and Industry: An Evaluation of Policy-related Research,* by William C. Gruben, and *An Evaluation of Policy-related Research on Fiscal Problems within the Urban Setting,* by Koren T. Sherrill.

I am indebted to Niles M. Hansen, director of the center, for his support in the organization of the research project. During the course of research I was assisted by John Vrooman and Luis Caso, graduate students in the Economics Department. I am also grateful for the support of John Surmeier of the National Science Foundation and of William Gruben, Koren Sherrill, Rita Ellison, and Pamela Pape, all patient research associates and fellow center staff.

The views expressed in the report are solely those of the author. They do not necessarily reflect those of the National Science Foundation or the Center for Economic Development.

The opportunity to turn from a relatively narrow focus on individual problems of urban economic development to a much more sweeping review has been an opportunity with mixed implications. On the one hand, it has required that I review literature once-noted but soon forgotten and that I reevaluate the residual impressions carried as vague notions from such encounters. The exercise has been stimulating. On the other hand, a review of the literature from the perspective of policy relevance has raised the frightening spectre that research in this area has too often proceeded in an amorphously cumulative fashion within which research effort has been directed and additions to knowledge have been made on the basis of considerations that only coincidentally reflect policy need.

The intent of this study has been more closely related to a reorganization within the frontiers of research than to a significant new effort to thrust them forward. If, however, the report serves to channel additional research effort into those least-charted areas of the policy-relevant research frontier that are identified and emphasized, and if it serves to reduce the many dimensions of the urban economic development problem to a conceptually manageable number for some planners, policy makers, and other concerned citizens, the effort will have been worthwhile.

1

Urban Growth versus Urban Economic Development: An Introduction

There may be no greater source of confusion in public debate about the relative merits of urban growth than that which results from the failure to distinguish between urban growth and urban economic development. *Urban growth* generally refers to increases in population within a specific urban area, increases in the number of jobs within that area, or increases in either the quantity or the value of the goods and services produced in a local economy. These quantitative changes do not necessarily lead to qualitative improvements in urban life. *Urban economic development* refers to increases in the quality of urban life associated with changes, not necessarily increases, in the size and composition of the population, the quantity and nature of local jobs, and the quantity and prices of goods and services produced locally. Analysis of urban economic development requires superimposition of value judgments with respect to the desirability of quantitative changes in the urban area. Here, urban economic development will refer to increases in the standard of living of those who live in an urban area as measured by the per capita level of income, the stability of income, and the distribution of income.

If one probes the reasons why many who advocate urban growth adopt such a position, one often finds that they are implicitly equating growth with development. If one probes the reasons why many opponents of growth take such a stance, one also finds an implicit assumption about the relationship between growth and development. Yet, urban economic development must be distinguished from urban growth. Growth may lead to development. But it is also possible that by slowing growth in, say, population one can increase the rate of development as measured, for example, by per capita income.

This report focuses on development, not growth; questions of growth are relegated to a subordinate position where, perhaps, they should remain. Our orientation, however, *is* toward those questions that underlie many growth controversies, for example:

What do you want from the economy of the urban area in which you live—higher average income, higher than that earned in other cities, or higher than that which you and your fellow citizens earned last year? Are your collective aspirations realistic? How can you know?

To what extent would you prefer a more stable local economy, with

1

fewer or smaller fluctuations in employment and income? What price must you pay to obtain it? To what extent is such stabilization feasible?

Can urban economic development proceed without conflicts among various interest groups or socioeconomic classes within cities? To what extent does urban economic development involve changing the distribution of benefits among residents of the city?

What, in fact, determines the level of economic development in one city compared with another? What, if anything, can be done to influence the quality of life in any specific city through local or locally initiated economic development programs?

This book offers the principal results of a year of research on the availability of answers to these questions and to others related to the economic structure of cities. The research, sponsored by the National Science Foundation through its division of Research Applied to National Needs (NSF-RANN), was undertaken for two reasons: (1) to make a significant body of policy-related research on municipal systems more accessible and usable for policy makers, and (2) to provide a more rigorous basis for future research projects dealing with policy-related research on municipal systems. It is our intention to provide a survey and a synthesis of the answers available at this time to the questions listed above and to indicate the large number of closely related questions that remain unanswered.

This study is designed to be as useful as possible to city officials, planners, concerned citizens, and students of urban life, who previously had little access to many of the studies considered here because they appeared solely in professional and academic journals or in largely technical books with limited circulation. The attempts by cities to influence the nature and direction of their economic development, attempts that are increasing in both their breadth and their intensity, have created an urgent need for better understanding of the processes involved. The proliferation of increasingly technical articles in increasingly obscure journals appears to be leading to an ever wider gap between the academic researchers concerned with urban problems and the planners who must absorb and apply the relevant results of that research.

The Intended Audience

City planners may now be the only professionals whom the public still expects to be "Renaissance men," that is, experts in all areas remotely related to their profession. Years ago local priests and ministers or local doctors were expected to have answers to all questions of psychology, politics, health, and the arts; for they were the only educated members of most communities. Today, most priests, ministers, and doctors have little hesitation to refer questions outside their own specialties to other specialized experts. City planners, however, are expected by elected officials and other citizens alike to be familiar with all the latest theories of urban growth, techniques for evaluating impacts, environmental approaches to land-use planning, and policies for stimulating local development. They are expected to foresee the urban future with enough accuracy to plan long-term, large-scale public investments. They are expected to foresee (and avoid) policies likely to stimulate political conflict. And they are even occasionally asked to comment on cultural and aesthetic endeavors, such as the advisability of using revenue-sharing funds for local ballet, theater, or other artistic programs.

It is hoped that this survey will lighten the load of city planners (with respect to all but, perhaps, the last problem) in at least two ways: First, by sorting through, evaluating, and synthesizing a large proportion of the available academic literature on urban economic development (more than 200 books, articles, and unpublished papers), the survey offers the city planner a relatively concise compendium of approaches to the problem to which he or she may turn when confronted with policy needs in the area. Second, the volume is deliberately written at a generally nontechnical level so that planners besieged by interested laymen inquiring about the seemingly incomprehensible complexities of urban development may refer them to an intelligible single source containing a broad summary.

The increasing level of citizen participation in city decision making raises this need for a nontechnical source of background information on urban economic development. The nature of urban economic development may be very complex, especially when considered from the point of view of a single city or metropolitan area set in a rapidly changing national economy. But the difficulty confronted by the interested layman who seeks to learn about the basic principles and the development alternatives available could be made far less forbidding than it frequently appears to be. Articles in most professional journals presuppose graduate-level training or years of experience in the relevant discipline. The jargon alone may make the article unintelligible to most. But the concepts involved are not so complex that no simplified presentation is possible.

If concerned citizens turn to other available books on the subject, they are apt to find three types available, none of which serve their purposes adequately. There are, first, the popular, easily readable essays, such as Jacobs' *The Economy of Cities* (1969), that provide engaging suggestions about the nature of urban economies and some fragmentory evidence to support the suggestions. Some such books are misleading, however; for they ignore or neglect much of the academic and professional research on cities done over the past forty years.

The second type of book that inquisitive individuals are likely to encounter are the professional monographs on various aspects of the urban economy or urban economies seen generally. These professional scientific studies, such as Otis Dudley Duncan, et al. (1960), Harvey S. Perloff, et al. (1960), Allen R. Pred (1966), or Wilbur R. Thompson (1965), have at least three liabilities when considered by the nonspecialized planner or the concerned layman. First, they frequently presuppose fairly extensive familiarity with urban economics or urban geography. Second, they require substantial investment of time and effort to obtain an understanding of what are often fairly narrow dimensions of urban economic development. And third, the nonprofessional reader is hard pressed to evaluate their contents or to relate their contents to other pertinent information in the field. This study attempts to remedy these difficulties and, in that way, to serve as a guide for policy makers who seek to inform themselves in a more detailed fashion about the problems that confront them.

There are also urban economics texts that have appeared with increasing frequency in the wake of the severe urban problems of the late 1960s and the demand that those problems created in the universities for urban economics courses. These texts, such as James Heilbrun (1973), Werner Z. Hirsch (1973), Douglas M. Brown (1974), Dick Netzer (1970), and Robert L. Bish and Robert J. Kirk (1974), are generally designed to serve purposes very different from those of this report. They tend, for example, to provide a broad discussion of many more dimensions of urban economics than this study. They tend to review professional research from the point of view of its contribution to the construction of theories or the testing of them, rather than from the point of view of policy relevance.

The texts are less than adequate for the purposes suggested here because, true to the traditional orientation of the professional researcher on urban economics in the past twenty years, they also tend to be oriented to the study of growth, rather than development. Most of the urban economics texts include chapters on the determinants of levels and rates of growth of population, jobs, or output. Few, however, contain detailed discussion of how those three dimensions of urban growth may be related to urban economic development.

The pioneering work by Wilbur R. Thompson, *A Preface to Urban Economics* (1965), was in fact the first detailed and explicit study of the nature of urban development as distinct from simple urban growth. This book represents, in many ways, a modest attempt to supplement and update Thompson's approach to the urban economy.

Organization of the Book

Chapters 2 through 6 of this book present a synthesis of the literature surveyed. Chapter 7 offers an agenda for priority future research in the area. For the sake of presenting the material as logically and as clearly as possible, the chapters are organized along topical or thematic lines. This organization means that some studies that deal with several or all of the various topics (e.g., Thompson [1965]) will be discussed partially in two or more chapters.

The organization of the individual chapters of the study largely follows the pattern established by Thompson. Chapter 2 offers an introduction to research on the determinants of the "economic structure" of urban areas from which the specific cities' economic development proceeds. *Economic structure,* as used here, refers to the distribution of the labor force or of value added [a] among industries of various sorts. *Industry* is used here in the broad sense, referring to the full spectrum of goods or services (retail trade or banking, as well as manufacturing). Although factors other than economic structure are considered, such as the age composition and skill levels of the local labor force and the availability of capital, the analysis of alternative development patterns and alternative development goals throughout this report focuses heavily upon the mix of industries that comprise the economic structure of the city. In Chapter 2 it is emphasized that the evolution of the structure of goods and services produced in each city must be viewed with respect to three overriding considerations: (a) the human, capital, and natural resources present in the metropolitan area at each moment; (b) the demand for those goods and services in the national and local economies; and (c) the continuous process of spatial competition among urban areas in the nation's urban system for the resources necessary to produce and for the markets for products.

The dynamism of the process that gives a city its structure at any moment is emphasized in order to note that it is *change* in the structure over time and not a measure of constancy that should be expected. Finally, the interrelatedness of all dimensions of the local urban economy and the national economy are stressed to provide a basis for the policy orientation of the succeeding chapters.

Chapters 3, 4, and 5 consider, in turn, the principal dimensions of urban economic development as suggested by Thompson. In Chapter 3

---

[a] *Value added* consists of the value of sales of a plant or a firm less the value of all products purchased by that firm from another firm and used as inputs. It offers a more accurate measure of the value of output across firms because double counting of those inputs is avoided.

recent research on the relationship between economic structure and the level and growth of per capita income in cities is synthesized. Alternative theoretical approaches to growth in employment and income are noted, and the persistent problem of relating such growth to the relevant measures of per capita welfare is noted. Export-base models are compared and contrasted in detail with neoclassical labor-supply analyses. An attempt is then made to distill from the limited number of available empirical studies some notion of the extent to which the alternative theoretical approaches are substantiated.

Chapter 4 focuses upon the problem of reducing instability in the urban economy. It draws rather heavily from the author's own work on the relationship between economic structure and the stability of income and employment. Substantial conflicts in theory and empirical evidence on the relationship between size, industrial diversity, growth rate, and stability are drawn together. Specific attention is given to whether diversification of the local economic structure is possible and, if so, how such might be accomplished. The relationship between different forms of growth and the stability of the economy also tends to emerge and is found to depend heavily on the economic structure of the individual city.

The distributional questions inherent in all economic development questions are considered in Chapter 5 in the context of urban economic development. Although there currently exist relatively few studies of the problems, the existence of differing effects across social and economic groups is implicit in several. Reevaluation of alternative development goals in terms of their likely distributional effects appears to shed light on important recent problems of urban conflict. The existence of differing distributional effects further highlights the need for public awareness and active public participation in urban development decisions. The most important recent study of the determinants of differences across local economies in the shape of the income distribution is found to be one that, once again, stresses the importance of the industrial structure of the urban economy. From that study we are able to derive suggestions as to the appropriate basis for analyzing the effect of different kinds of growth upon income distribution.

One of the principal conclusions that emerges from each of Chapters 2 through 5 is that detailed knowledge of the strengths and weaknesses of the local urban economy is the most important prerequisite to the design of an urban development policy. Chapter 6 responds to the question, "How can the development prospects of an area be determined?" Three major studies of the characteristics of local area economies are compared and contrasted. The first two, the "New York Metropolitan Region Study" and the "Economic Study of the Pittsburgh Region" are classic examples of highly professional, well-organized attempts to discern the workings of metropolitan area economies in the context of the changing national economy. The third, a set of studies of the Nova Scotia economy by Stanislaw Czamanski, offers a comparable analysis of a regional economy that demonstrates the use of some more sophisticated techniques for approaching the same problem. Among the three studies and the three economies studied we find a wide range of techniques used, conclusions drawn, and implications for developmental policy laid out.

The final chapter draws together key findings and suggests areas for priority new research.

2 What Determines the Economic Structure of a City?

The urban economy consists of an ever-changing, complexly interrelated group of economic activities that take place within a relatively small area. The external characteristics of those activities—factories, warehouses, homes, roads, jobs, incomes, unemployment, poverty, or wealth—that we see in the city are created by the production of goods and services in that area both for residents of that city and for those who live elsewhere in the nation or the world. The conscious development of that urban economy consists of creating policies designed to alter the quantity or the composition of the goods and services produced there in order to accomplish specific goals.

To determine whether the goals of an urban economic development program are feasible and, if feasible, to determine how they might be accomplished, we first need to acquire at least a rudimentary understanding of the principal influences that have tended to shape the urban economy at the outset. If we ignore the basic determinants of the economy of a given city, the possibility is increased considerably that we will design a completely unrealistic or utopian development program or that we will adopt policies that will worsen, rather than improve, the health of the urban economy.

The economic forces that continually shape and reshape the structure of the urban economy are the subject of this chapter. We approach the analysis of those forces in four ways: First, we consider some of the overriding general characteristics of the urban economy that should be kept in mind when tracing the historical development of the economy of any given city. Second, we examine a very simple illustrative example of the early formation of a hypothetical city; the example will serve to introduce the principal considerations that run through the chapter. We then consider some of the evidence available on the extent to which the actual evolution of American cities has reflected the general characteristics and the simplified model presented. Finally, we conclude by considering each of the principal determinants of economic location among cities and by evaluating some of the current literature on the nature and relative importance of each.

The urban economy consists of production processes that have five general characteristics: The economy is, first, open to the movement of

9

products, people, and capital. Unlike the national economy, which is protected from some of the jarring aspects of such movements by customs regulations, immigration procedures, and controls on capital flows, the urban economy is open to the beneficial aspects of and vulnerable to the damaging aspects of such movements. To the extent that such movements take place, the urban economy must adapt rapidly or suffer erratic swings in the products, jobs, and income that it produces.

The urban economy must also be seen as a general equilibrium phenomenon. *General equilibrium* may be defined as a specific state of an economic system in which the identifiable desires of men and the obstacles to their fulfillment have reached a balance.[a] The desires that enter the urban economy are all those aspirations of producers and consumers alike that determine their location and level of production or consumption. The obstacles to fulfillment are the same scarcities of human and natural resources, capital, and income that constrain production and consumption decisions in the nonspatial economy, plus the additional costs of transportation from one point to another and the ultimate scarcity of land at the center of any population concentration.

In fundamentally "market" economies such as most in Western Europe and the Western Hemisphere, the principal mechanism for achieving general equilibrium in the urban economy is the markets that exist for products and factors of production in each city. The markets with respect to which the economic structure of any city will tend to be in balance are not only the local markets for products, labor, and capital, but also regional, national, and international markets for the products produced in the city, for the labor of people who reside in the city, or for the capital needed to produce in the city. The general equilibrium approach thus requires analysis of influences far beyond any specific city to understand the past, present, and future of the city's economic structure.

The processes that govern the level of economic activity in cities are also *simultaneous* by which we mean that we cannot isolate simple chains of causation between one change in the urban economy and all of its direct and indirect causes or effects. Each change in the urban economy is caused by a complex web of national, regional, and local forces that converge simultaneously to lead to the change in question. On the one hand, this characteristic could be taken as justification for the complex, confusing, and even contradictory interpretations of the urban economy given by some urban specialists. On the other hand, it provides a small indication of the enormous complexity of the social system we are analyzing when we try to understand the economies of cities.

The urban economy is also *dynamic,* by which we are not suggesting

---

[a] Nontechnical introductions to the concept of general equilibrium as applied to cities and regions may be found in David F. Bramhall (1969).

that it is necessarily powerful—the literal meaning of the term; the technical meaning given by economists and other social scientists is that such systems are closely related to time; they are, more specifically, continually changing through time. That cities are constantly changing is obvious. What is not so obvious is that the determinants of their economic structures are continually changing and that, therefore, the actual economic structures should be changing. One implication of the dynamic nature of urban development processes is that some industries will shrink and disappear and others may take their place. Some cities will shrink and some will grow; over time the roles may be reversed. These patterns are not the fault of the industries, the cities, or the officials of one or the other, nor can such changes be prevented in many cases.

That the urban economic system is considered dynamic might seem to conflict with the notion that the urban economy is a general equilibrium phenomenon. There is no conflict; there is only greater complexity. For the economy of the city, as it tends toward general equilibrium, is, in fact, "shooting at a moving target." Every change over time in the determinants of the economic structure alters the nature of the balances that would bring equilibrium to the full set of urban markets. That is, changes in the urban economy during 1974 to adjust to changes in the determinants that occurred in 1973 may not be precisely the changes that would be needed to adjust to 1974 changes in the determinants. The urban economy is constantly adjusting and readjusting itself to changes in the forces that mold it.

Finally, we should also note that the economic structures of cities have stochastic or probabilistic characteristics. At any moment we cannot know with certainty just what the industrial composition is, just what it will be, or, much less, just what it should be to accomplish any developmental goals. We can know with some precision what the economic structure once was by conducting employment or production surveys. We can know with some precision how some industries will grow for a few months into the future by surveying plant managers on their firms' plans. But the uncertainty that characterizes our knowledge beyond that, uncertainty about even the most important determinants of urban economic structure, such as the future state of the national economy, future costs of transportation, or future demographic trends, makes the formulation of urban economic development policy even more hazardous than was suggested previously by the complexity of the urban economy.

What Leads to the Creation of Cities?

Classical location theory, associated with Johann Heinrich Von Thünen (1826), Alfred Weber (1929), Walter Christaller (1966), and August

Loesch (1964), identified two principal economic forces that would tend to lead persons to leave isolated subsistence farms and to gather together into communities, towns, and cities. They are (1) the economies of scale that are present in the production of many products, and (2) the economies associated with reducing distance between related production processes. *Economies of scale* refer to the reduction in cost per unit of production that occurs when the scale of production is increased. Economies of scale exist in almost every production process, are seen most frequently in manufactured goods, and even appear for many services. The production of one-of-a-kind artwork may be the principal exception. Economies of reduced distance may be taken to mean that shipping is rarely costless and that reductions in shipping costs may mean reductions in the final costs of products. More importantly, where shipping or other impersonal means of covering distance is not possible, the cost of moving people from job to job, from home to job, from home to store, or from store to store is reduced significantly by locating jobs, homes, and stores near one another.

Let us illustrate some of these relationships and introduce some additional basic ideas by means of a simplified example of community formation. Assume that at one time there existed a large group of primarily self-sufficient primitive farmers who lived on isolated individual farms spread over a series of rolling hills and river-laced valleys far from any urbanized areas. In some ways this setting could be taken from the Australian "outback" or from the frontier American Midwest, but let us not date the setting. If one of those farmers was to realize that there existed economies of scale in the production of farm implements for himself and for his neighbors, specialized manufacturing activity would be introduced into the economy of the area. How many farm implements would that new specialist ultimately make? That would depend upon several things: (1) how much more cheaply he could make the implements than his neighbors if they each made their own; (2) how much it cost to ship the finished implements from his plant to the neighbors' farms; (3) how long the implements lasted; and (4) how densely the area around the implement maker was settled.[b]

Look closely at some of the relationships between some of these determinants of the size of his output. First, even if he could produce the implements for virtually nothing, there would exist some distance beyond which it would not pay other farmers to purchase implements from this central producer. The costs of shipping, no matter how low, would at

---

[b] Excellent summaries of the economic concepts involved in market area analysis may be found in Hugh O. Nourse (1968), Brian J. L. Berry (1967), and Peter E. Lloyd and Peter Dicken (1972).

some point exceed the costs of manufacturing the implements at home. This distance beyond which none of the products of a plant tend to be sold may be used to define the outer boundary of a market area for products produced at one point, in this case farm implements. The quantity of implements that would be produced for farmers in the market area would then be limited by the number of farmers specifically within the market area.

If we assume that the economies of scale were fairly substantial and the costs of shipping fairly small, then it is conceivable that a large number of farm implements would be produced, perhaps more than the single, former farmer and his family could produce alone. To the extent that he then needs to hire labor, it is reasonable to expect that his laborers will try to live close to their place of work. Laborers who are not farmers need to have their food needs provided by those who are farmers, and the group of homes clustered about the farm implements factory becomes a logical place for the location of a general store to serve as middleman between farmers and laborers. Thus, the service industry is born in the new central place.

The general store is also likely to draw customers from the neighboring farms. As individual farmers become more specialized in both their basic products and in the products, such as hams, salt beef, and dried or preserved fruits and vegetables, which represent small-scale home food processing, they will begin to rely more on the general store for the products they are no longer producing for themselves. The market area for the general store would tend to vary with the nature of the products it stocks. Hams, salt beef, and preserves might draw farmers from long distances, if the economies of scale in specialized home processing are considerable and if travel costs are low. Products such as fresh bread, fruit, or vegetables, which do not ship well, would have considerably reduced market areas.

Note that now the community or central place has several market areas that determine how much will be manufactured and sold within it. These market areas also determine, to a certain extent, the number of persons who can be supported by the community economy. That is, the various market areas determine, to some extent, the size of the community.

Will the market areas also determine the income level of the community? Yes, to some extent, as we can see. Prior to the opening of the farm implements factory, farming in the area and home processing for trade among the neighbors provided the principal (if not the only) sources of income for farm families. Unless new laborers migrated to the area, the owner of the plant would have to offer wages at least equal to average farm wages to draw labor out of agriculture and into industry. If the income of the remaining farmers rises as some farmers shift to factory work (because, for example, those who remain have more land with which to work), then each additional factory worker will require a higher wage. Both farm and nonfarm incomes will rise. If the farm implements factory is able to introduce new processes for making its products that permit even greater economies of scale or other cost reductions and, consequently, lower prices at the plant, then the market area will be expanded; more farm implements will be sold; the community may grow and incomes may rise.

The relatively cautious nature of these conclusions is necessary, for we have omitted one important element from the fable—the rest of the world. What has been happening in the rest of the world, the rest of the farming world, for example, into which the farm implements market area is supposedly expanding. It is reasonable to expect that somewhere, out there, some other mechanically inclined farmer is going to realize that he can improve his lot by specializing in mass production of farm implements. This is more likely in areas outside the market area of the first producer or toward the outer edges of that market area where shipping costs are relatively high. Unless the first producer has some basis for monopoly control over his market area (e.g., an important patent), he must expect the growth of competing factories around and partially overlapping his original market area. The new boundary will occur where delivered prices from the two plants are just equal, for on either side of that point all purchases will be made from the plant that can deliver for less.

Market area competition introduces two new consequences: First, it is also likely that a community or town will grow around the second factory, that the community will develop service industries of its own, and that some of those service industries will compete with the services provided in the first town. Growth in both size and income levels is now competitive between these young towns. Improved production techniques in one will mean expansion of its market areas, expanded output, expanded employment, and possibly expanded income. And that growth will come at the cost of output, employment, and income in the competing towns whose economic structure is more or less based on the same industries.

Whether the expanded output leads to sustained increases in income in the town where it takes place depends principally on two items: (1) the availability of additional labor force in town, and (2) the amount of migration that takes place.[c] Expanded output will lead to increased wage levels only if there is not enough labor available in the same town or from migration to fill the expanded employment requirements. If expansion of employment, the labor force, and migration occur continually, it is only

---

[c] Detailed discussion of these interrelationships occur later in this chapter in connection with evaluation of the study by Richard F. Muth (1969).

necessary that employment expansion proceed more rapidly than the combined local labor force expansion plus migration in order to generate rising wages.

The Generation of a "System" of Cities

Let's assume that a few years have passed since the onset of urbanization in the mythical region with which we began. Now, as we return, we find that some towns are growing more rapidly than others. Why is this? If we look closely we may find that one of the early manufacturing sites was coincidentally located at a crossroads and a ford in a major river. The presence of the river made it possible for a water-powered grist mill and sawmill to locate there. The presence of the crossroads and ford brought many travelers to the town and encouraged the growth of services oriented to them. And perhaps the initial factory has outcompeted its regional rivals to the extent that it serves a very large market area, employs many workers, and has even led to the location nearby of related factories making inputs for the farm implements.

Would this have meant the death of the towns that were outcompeted in terms of farm implements? Not necessarily. At least two possibilities remain for economic structures there. First, the closing of their farm implements plants would have left a relatively skilled labor force in the area that would take some years to migrate away. If a firm in some other industry that can use labor of approximately that type learned of the availability of the local labor force, that town might be chosen as the site for another plant. But such fairy-tale conclusions are rare and unlikely, even in this fable. It is more likely that the loss of the major industry would lead to the migration of its employees and to a reduction in the size of the town.

Would this imply permanent reduction in per capita income? Not necessarily, for if the migration of the labor force to areas of better employment opportunity took place sufficiently rapidly, the average income of those who remained need not have fallen. Only if the plant that closed employed a large proportion of the labor force and paid higher than average wages might average incomes have fallen.

How much would the town shrink in population? If we consider the case of a town like those described above, that had only a few industries, it would shrink to the point where its population could be supported by the market areas of its remaining industries.

Communities that provide limited numbers of economic functions to relatively small hinterlands may come about more frequently through growth processes that never included major functions with large market areas. These are the towns that "fill in" the landscape between the major cities and that provide locally the goods and services that the major city cannot provide because distances exceed the radius of the respective market areas.[d]

Over the years the cities in the region might tend to grow into a "system" of cities with some evidence of an "urban hierarchy." This system would consist of interrelationships among cities and towns such that economic functions with the largest market areas are provided from a single city to all of the cities within the area. Each of the cities thus served would provide services with smaller market areas to the areas around them. If the economic functions with largest market areas tend to cluster in a single city and if functions with smaller market areas cluster in a small number of outlying cities, an urban hierarchy will be created in which the most complex economic structure is associated with the largest city and a generally regular gradation of economic structures and sizes from largest and most complex to smallest and least complex may be found.

The fabled initial communities and the fabled system of cities may have served to illustrate some rudimentary relationships between economic structure and urban growth in a theoretical competitive context; but what relationship, if any, do these simplified examples have to the actual economic development and the current competitive structure of the system of cities in the United States in the mid-1970s?

What Factors Have Led to U.S. Urban Economic Structures?

The historical bases for the growth of urban economies in the United States have been examined most extensively by Eric E. Lampard (1955, 1968) and Allan R. Pred (1966). Important studies of more narrow scope have been contributed by Carl H. Madden (1956a, 1958). The broad contemporary relationships between economic structure and the urban system have been described by Otis Dudley Duncan, et al. (1960), and Beverly Duncan and Stanley Lieberson (1970).

Eric Lampard, the noted economic historian, has traced the principal

---

[d] Emphasis has been given here to the shrinking of towns in the evaluation of urban systems because such phenomena and their effects (migration from small towns to large, substantial redevelopment efforts, and acrimony over the causes of the declining population) have received considerable attention recently. It is perhaps more important to understand the development issues related to declining urban populations that those related to growing populations, for more public funds are likely to be misspent on the former than on the latter.

urbanization tendencies in the more developed countries in general (1955) and in the United States in particular (1968). He notes in the earlier study that the simultaneous growth of cities, population, and nonagricultural employment "seems to have been a characteristic feature of all economically advancing societies." He later asserts, even more strongly:

> The mere presence of large cities in a region does not . . . ensure the existence of a developed economy. But it is no less clear that developed economies do not occur anywhere in the world without the presence of a large population specialized away from subsistence agriculture, and residing in a "hierarchy" of different-sized cities ranging from one (or more) metropolitan centers at the peak to a broad base of medium and small-sized cities with less than 100,000 inhabitants.

Lampard attempted an appraisal of the specific role that cities have played in the dramatic evolution of the economically advanced areas. Drawing more from intuition than from historical data, he suggested that increases in productive effeciency have been the most important sources of the improvement of the quality of life in the more developed nations, that specialization and the division of labor have been the principal sources of improved efficiency, and, finally, that specialization implies spatial concentration and is reinforced by spatial concentration of the economy into cities.

Thirteen years later he undertook a much more thorough analysis of urbanization and development in the United States. For this latter study he prepared extensive analyses of census data for the period from 1790 through 1960. The relationship between industrialization (movement into nonagricultural employment) and urbanization did not appear so clear. The rate at which the labor force has been transformed from agricultural to nonagricultural employment fluctuates much more erratically than the relatively high and constant rate of urbanization in the United States. The pattern in New England and the Middle Atlantic states appears particularly troublesome. "Clearly," Lampard noted, referring to the early nineteenth century, "the labor force in some of the Northeastern states was industrialized in the present sense without benefit of sustained urbanization and much of its market was, doubtless, to be found within the local agricultural stratum as well as in the towns of adjacent states" (1968, p. 122). In this century he finds that the relative poverty persisting in the regions with low urbanization and low labor force industrialization levels is now "no less apparent."

The evolution of a system of cities, he suggested, can be seen in the geographic distribution of the largest cities across the country at various points during the past 170 years and in the extent to which the cumulative distribution of cities by size has remained remarkably constant over time. Overall, he concluded, "The elements of structure and stability to be found in the evolving system of cities are broadly consistent with the notions of central place theory" (1968, p. 135).

Carl H. Madden contributed three path-breaking analyses of spatial and temporal aspects of the growth of cities across the United States (1956a, 1956b, and 1958). He found evidence for a rather impressive consistency in the size-distribution of cities, evidence of clear competition for growth, and even some evidence of the long-term impact of that competition upon cities at different distances from major metropolitan centers that support the urban hierarchy notion.

Madden examined the growth histories of all 106 United States cities with populations in excess of 100,000 as of 1950 and all 339 United States cities of 10,000 or more in 1950 "which were reported continuously in the census for a century." He found that from 1850 to 1950 there had been a pervasive tendency toward declining average percentage rates of growth in each decade and in every region, although identical long-term average growth rates have seemed to result from differing growth tendencies on the part of individual cities from decade to decade. United States urban growth, he reported, has consistently been most rapid in younger cities and has tended to move across the country with the spread of population. Not one of the sixty-nine cities over 100,000 in 1950, reported in the census since 1950, and growing faster than ten percent per decade from 1850 to 1950, for example, was located in the northeast. He suggested that the westward movement of the population led to the creation of "substitute service centers" to replace older ones farther east. "Throughout the nineteenth century," he surmised, "the relative gain of the cities in states farther west was the relative loss of the cities in states farther east (1958, p. 164).

In a separate study (1956b) Madden analyzed size and rates of growth per decade of all cities over 10,000 from 1790 to 1950 and took special note of the significance of the distance of each of 1262 cities from sixty-seven major metropolitan centers. He found that the median size of cities does not decline uniformly as one moves away from the metropolitan areas. Rather, as one would expect from a system of cities providing specialized functions, "the median size of the places in the 45 to 64 mile zone has been consistently larger than it is in the next nearer and next farther distance zones" (p. 379). That is, there has tended to be a belt of medium-sized second-echelon cities at a relatively constant distance from major cities, presumably to supply a consistent set of secondary economic functions to market areas outside the areas for those functions as provided by the major cities. The space between these cities and the major cities was "filled-in" by smaller places providing functions with even smaller market areas and tending, for that reason, to be smaller. Madden also encountered that the growth rates of the cities in the forty-five to sixty-four mile belt tended to slow down at about the same rate as the major metropolitan areas. Those places on either side of that belt tended to decline in growth more rapidly than the second-echelon cities, presumably reflecting a gradual erosion of their market areas to the larger cities.

Madden demonstrated clearly that there was marked stability over time in the size distribution of cities—the shape of the system as a whole (1956a), but similar *instability* in the place of individual cities within that system. He noted, adamantly:

> . . . A progressive economy is always characterized by differences in the rates of development of its individual cities. Progress in the economy is marked by new inventions, changes in the methods of production, the discovery of new commodities, sources of raw materials, and such developments. These developments have "served to stimulate or depress, but to an unequal extent, the development of various industries." [e] Similarly, this progress has also served to stimulate or depress, but to an unequal extent, the growth of various cities [1958, p. 146].

Further emphasizing the changing history of the 106 individual large cities over the century of observation, he noted that "there is no indication among these large cities of any tendency for a city to reach a certain size and stay at the same size" (p. 169).

Madden had little empirical basis for asserting the relationship he claimed between technological change and relative urban growth. Allan R. Pred, however, has provided detailed consideration of these factors in a landmark study of changing urban-industrial growth from 1800 to 1914 (1966). Pred suggests that industrialization, and especially the concentration of industrial production in relatively few plants located in a few principal cities, was the most important source of urban growth in the 1860 to 1914 period. Prior to that time, the most rapidly growing cities were commercial cities within which manufacturing grew only as a gradual substitute for the imported products upon which commerce was based.

For the 1860 to 1914 urban-industrial growth period, Pred has developed a model of growth that adds three important dimensions to our simple model above. He suggests that in the context of individual cities competing for growth, the winners have enjoyed three basic characteristics, all compounded by the effects of innovation: First, they have enjoyed some basic "initial advantage," whether location at a favorable transport site or the early expansion of a rapidly growing industry. This initial ad-

[e] A. F. Burns, *Production Trends in the United States Since 1870* (New York: National Bureau of Economic Research, 1934), p. 65.

vantage, he believes, is reinforced by the external economies or "agglom-eration economies" that reduce the cost of production for some or all pro-ducers who locate there simply because other producers are already there. It is further reinforced by cumulative "threshold effects" under which growth in the city from the location of one firm expands the local market enough to permit location of another unrelated firm oriented to market size. This process of "cumulative and circular causation" is then, Pred claims, further aided by a direct relationship that he demonstrates between size and rate of growth and inventive activity as measured by patents granted.

Pred supports the notion that industrial growth was the major source of urban growth during that period by noting, among other evidence, that of the eleven currently most important industrial metropolises, ten experi-enced the largest absolute increases in population of any cities in the United States between 1860 and 1910. He supports the influence of inven-tion by noting that the same eleven cities accounted for thirty-two percent of the nation's patents in 1960 while they contained less than thirteen per-cent of the population. The ratio of patents per capita in those cities to patents per capita in the nation is also almost perfectly correlated with city size. Exceptions seem correlated with rates of growth (higher rates of growth creating conditions for more rapid innovation). So Pred concludes that "the locational configuration of inventive and innovative activities is some function of both the size and rate of growth of cities" (p. 112).

In summary, the growth of cities in the United States appears to be closely related to industrial structure in ways generally reflected by our simplified central place illustration. The overall urban system has main-tained rather striking stability, but individual cities have varied significantly in their histories within that system. During the period of most clearly marked urban-industrial growth, the interrelationships between initial ad-vantage, threshold sizes, agglomeration economies, and the reinforcement of invention and industrial concentration enabled the nation's largest in-dustrial cities to outcompete their rivals.

The principal source of employment growth in the last forty years, however, has been growth in the services. Do the same phenomena apply to the service sectors? What characteristics may be seen in the economic structures of large and rapidly growing cities in more recent years?

Do These Patterns Apply to Contemporary Cities?

We do not have comprehensive studies of the determinants of very recent relative urban growth, but two fairly recent studies have helped to extend the analysis above through the 1950s. Otis Dudley Duncan, W. Richard

Scott, Stanley Lieberson, Beverly Duncan and Hal H. Winsborough published in 1960 (Duncan, et al. 1960) a monumental analysis of the nature of metropolises, their roles in the national economy, and their relations to their regional economies. They attempted to establish a "mid-century bench mark" as evidence of the evolution of the nation's largest cities and of their industrial structures as basis for future analysis of the evolution of cities and of the urban system in the United States. Their methodology was largely ecological. That is, they sought to view the cities in the urban system "in terms of their place in a total ecosystem, the major facets of which are populations adjusting to their environments by means of their technological equipment and patterns of social organization" (p. 3).

To accomplish this they examined first the theoretical literature available on large cities and their functions, considered the theoretical relationships between metropolises and their regional hinterlands or principal market areas and resource supply areas, and then analyzed the fifty largest United States cities in 1950 in terms of these considerations. The metropolis, to them, was an urban place that was very large by its nature, though not by definition. It contained large-scale manufacturing functions, but it tended to be distinguished more by the provision of financial and commercial services to a large regional hinterland. As Beverly Duncan later noted (Duncan and Lieberson 1970, pp. 18–21), "when the study was completed, the formulations of metropolitan structure distilled from the literature seemed less cogent than they had at the outset. Not every large population center need be a 'metropolis' nor need the 'metropolitan region' be relevant to all the functions carried out in a center. . . ." Duncan et al. found that they could divide the fifty largest cities (after New York and Chicago) into five categories on the basis of their relationships to their regions, the manufacturing and commercial functions they performed, and the resultant characteristics of their economic structures:

1. Metropolitan centers with diversified manufacturing and metropolitan functions (Boston, Pittsburgh, St. Louis, Cleveland, Buffalo, and Cincinnati)
2. Metropolitan centers with primarily regional metropolitan functions (San Francisco, Kansas City, Dallas, Denver, and others)
3. Regional capitals that are primarily oriented to smaller local areas, though they may perform some national manufacturing and service functions (Houston, New Orleans, Indianapolis, Richmond, and others)
4. Diversified manufacturing centers (Baltimore, Milwaukee, Toledo, and others)
5. Specialized manufacturing (Providence, Dayton, Akron, and others)

Their analysis of the relationship of the economic structures of these cities led them to several conclusions relevant to our analysis.

1. It appears to be a workable hypothesis that nearly every city has a more or less standard repertoire of functions performed for its own inhabitants and for its immediate continuous "hinterland"—comprising the area which it serves and upon which it depends most closely, in conformity with the central place scheme. But many cities have highly distinctive functions that make up important parts of their economic base and that involve them in ramified relationships with a variety of "regions" [p. 5].

2. [T]he urban hierarchy in the United States, as far as manufacturing is concerned, is a truly national one. In regard to services, however, it may be meaningful to think of broad regions as having more or less self-contained hierarchies of cities. . . . [p. 7].

3. [C]ertain aspects of the variation of industry composition with city size . . . call for explanatory principles other than those supplied by the centrality principle. Apparently, large cities generate certain distinctive types of needs or demands, which are then satisfied locally by specialized economic units [p. 7].

They also found that the market area or hinterland notion was far more relevant to service functions than to manufacturing.

The study by Duncan and Lieberson (1970) is offered by the authors as a sequel to Duncan et al. The latter was oriented to a cross-section analysis as of 1950. It emphasized analysis of the relationship between city size, location in the national hierarchy, and economic structure at one point in time. Duncan and Lieberson offer a set of essays related more to the development history of economic structures. Borrowing heavily from Duncan et al. for both hypotheses and methodology, they offer brief descriptions of the mercantile bases of colonial cities, the transformation of some of them into industrial cities by 1900, and detailed studies of the industrial structure of the eighteen largest cities in 1900. The study suffers from some noncontinuity between essays and from the unwillingness of the authors to present summaries of their observations or to help the reader draw inferences. They extend their analysis to some extent up to the 1960s, but the discussion is not conducted along parallel lines.

Their two most important conclusions with respect to contemporary growth of cities seem to be (1) that cities which are now growing rapidly relative to most have different economic structures than those places which grew rapidly in the past, and (2) that the most prominent dimension of these differences in economic structure is seen in the manufacturing sector, where new lines of industry tend to be distributed territorially more or less independently of the older industries that formed the principal bases for expansion of the nation's major cities in the past.

From the point of view of local area economic development, these conclusions would seem to be encouraging. For they suggest that the self-reinforcing growth of the traditional industrial cities, which Pred described, is not capturing all new industry and that the growth of other cities that have not previously possessed a strongly growing industrial base is still a possibility, if it is desired. These conclusions also raise the necessity of analyzing very carefully the locational advantages and disadvantages of any given city and the factors that determine the location of new or expanded industries within the current complex urban system.

Principal Factors Affecting Contemporary Industrial Location

The theoretical literature identifies four factors related to production costs and two overlapping considerations from the demand side: (1) transportation costs of supplies to a plant and of products from a plant to markets, (2) relative labor costs, (3) external economies of agglomeration, and (4) availability of natural resources. These factors all tend to vary in differing degrees from site to site. The relative level of demand for products will be determined largely by market potential, and a combination of the size and relative income of the population in an area. Each of these factors has received considerable attention in recent years. We discuss here just the major dimensions of each factor and some of the recent studies of each.

The costs of shipping supplies or products is likely to dominate the location decision of a plant only in those cases where they are very significant proportions of the total price paid by the purchaser. Sand and gravel are good examples. The location of iron ore enrichment plants at the site of the mine reflect the transport costs saved by shipping only the enriched products. In general, the reduction in transport costs is only one factor that the producer must integrate into his location decision, but it appears to be a significant one for determining both the national structure of individual industries and the spatial distribution of those industries across the nation.

The relative magnitude of "transport inputs," as they are called by Walter Isard (1956), determines to a large extent whether an industry is transport-oriented rather than labor-oriented. If labor costs do not vary substantially among alternative locations or if they are a small proportion of total costs, then an industry may be considered *transport-oriented,* and its location decision will be made on the basis of the relative transport costs of inputs and products. In general, since supplies may be of many sorts and may come from many places and since products may be shipped to many markets, the transport-oriented industry does not yield any simple general solution for the location of all individual firms.

Transportation costs, however, and changes over time in those costs as new modes of transport arise have had substantial impacts on the growth of regions and of cities within regions in the United States. Benjamin Chinitz has identified two long historical phases in the influence of transportation costs upon regional and urban growth (Chinitz 1960a). The first, which he dubs the "centralization" phase, coincided with the early development of the railroads and the consequent enormous reduction in overland freight rates. This reduction in transport costs, Chinitz believes, permitted the singular concentration of industries in very large-scale plants serving enormous market areas within the nation or the nation as a whole. Since 1929, however, Chinitz believes that the regional shift of manufacturing to the South and West is related to transport cost factors that reduced the trend toward concentration. Industries that have relatively high freight costs have been less able to counter these costs with economies of scale from concentrated production and have been more responsive to the decentralization trend. The introduction of truck hauling and the generally greater advantages associated with short-haul trucking, according to Chinitz, have all tended to encourage the movement of plants closer to markets.

Marvin J. Barloon has suggested that this trend may have continued to the point that "it may be said that transportation requirements are of little, or of limited, influence in the selection of industrial locations with respect to a growing portion of the periodic increment to the nation's industrial establishment (Barloon 1965, p. 169). He argues that the trend toward ever more finished products carries with it the implication that general bulk shipments of virtually unprocessed products are of less significance. The more finished products require specialized shipping services that are increasingly available everywhere and thus distance is of much lower significance. Barloon does not offer quantitative substantiation of his hypotheses, but the suggestions appear basically plausible. It would be valuable to know the specific industries most likely to be increasingly "footloose" and to know the relative magnitude of their output nationwide, but he offers no suggestion other than to imply that they are significant.

The most recent survey of the literature in this area is a study by Gerald Kraft, John R. Meyer, and Jean-Paul Valette (1971). Their study was undertaken "to determine to what extent economists have answered the question of whether, how, and by how much transportation affects regional development." They survey the principal theories, consider the empirical studies that have been done in the United States, and derive conclusions similar to those of Barloon. Changing transport costs and modes have been both a direct and an indirect cause of industrial decentralization away from the regions of initial concentration. They also suggest that the decreasing share of transport costs in final sales prices and the changing composition of goods shipped imply that transport costs will be much less influential in location decisions in the future. They examine current technological change in the various transport modes, ask whether any specific modes (and, therefore, any particular regions) are likely to be favored, and they conclude that there is no evidence that technological change will give significant advantage to any mode. The state of the art with respect to the locational attraction of transportation systems within cities is, they indicate, "not sufficiently advanced" to offer conclusive evidence beyond general conclusions that congested systems are unattractive.

The differences in the cost of labor in different urban areas is frequently cited as an important determinant of the movement and relative expansion of industry. There are numerous qualifications that must be attached to the concept of labor costs, and it would serve us well to clarify the concept before proceeding further. It is necessary to note first that cheap labor is not necessarily labor that is paid low wages. Labor must be measured, or thought of, in "efficiency" terms. If the difference in efficiency between low wage and high wage labor is greater than the difference in wages, the high wage labor would be "cheaper." Efficiency must also be viewed over a period. Low-wage employees with high absenteeism or high turnover may tend to be less efficient overall than higher wage employees with comparable hourly efficiency but better average efficiency over time. Finally, wage differentials, efficiency, and worker habits are also reflected in the average cost of any training required. On the job training may offset low initial efficiency of low-wage workers, but that training may become expensive (raising average labor costs) if turnover is high. It is, therefore, the long-term average cost per efficiency unit of labor that firms are likely to consider.

The best study to date of the magnitude of wage differentials by region and city was done by Victor R. Fuchs (1967).[f] In that study Fuchs used the 1/1000 sample from the 1960 census and derived estimates of actual earnings per hour for 56,247 individuals in 168 age, sex, race, and education groups. If we can assume that those 168 groups will tend to differentiate the relative efficiency of the members of each group, standardizing for the age, sex, race, and educational composition of regional and urban populations affords one way of adjusting the labor force for differing efficiency. Fuchs calculated expected earnings for five major regions and for an unspecified number of cities, divided into six size classes.

---

[f] Other studies that have been largely superseded by Fuchs are Richard A. Lester (1945, 1946, and 1947) and S. C. Sufrin, et al. (1948).

Expected earnings consisted of the average earnings that would have been encountered in the region or city if each laborer in its population had been paid the national average wages corresponding to his or her age, sex, race, and educational group.

Hourly earnings, when adjusted in that way for efficiency show significant differentials across regions and across cities of different size. Earnings were significantly lower in the South (by about twenty-five percent) than in other regions; earnings in the West were slightly higher than in the Northeast or North Central divisions. After standardizing for differences in age, sex, race, and education, the differential between the South and the rest of the country is about seventeen percent. A strong and consistently positive relationship was found by Fuchs between earnings and city size in every region and for every race and sex group. After also adjusting for differences in average city sizes in the different regions, the South still had about nine percent lower wages. Differences in actual average hourly earnings across cities of different size were twelve percent for all cities and from fifty-three percent in the South to twenty-six percent in the West. Regression analysis suggested that these differences were not significantly related to extent of unionization, although the general South/non-South differential is related to unionization.

Fuchs was unable to find statistical bases for explaining the large remaining city size differentials. He hypothesized, however, that they reflect "differences in quality not captured by standardization for color, age, sex, and education. This might take the form of better quality schooling [though the same number of years], more on-the-job training, selective in-migration to big cities of more ambitious and hard-working persons, or other forms" (p. 34). We shall consider an alternative explanation more thoroughly in the next chapter: disequilibrium in the markets for labor and capital such that the demand for labor, given the availability of capital, is persistently greater than the supply of labor in the larger cities.

Further dimensions of labor factors in the industrial development of the South were considered by Frank T. de Vyver in an earlier article, which also sheds light on more complex dimensions of labor costs and the labor factor in location (de Vyver 1951). De Vyver indicated that one should expect southern wages to be lower than northern for several reasons: the lower wages associated with the tendency toward smaller cities, the concealed unemployment in agriculture, and the industrial mix favoring low productivity employment. He then proceeded to suggest additional labor cost considerations that would make the Southern location attractive for labor-oriented industries. The weakness of southern labor organization, as reflected in estimated union membership in some key industries, provides new or relocated industries considerable respite from the direct and indirect costs of dealing with the unions. Lower costs for workmen's compensation insurance and other generally looser labor legislation in the South lessen indirect costs there.

A third location factor frequently cited in the literature and potentially capable of explaining some of the city size differentials in wages are the so-called "agglomeration economies." As noted by Hugh O. Nourse, the name *agglomeration* comes from the agglomeration or concentration of people in one place because of employment opportunities (Nourse 1968). Agglomeration economies are divided by Nourse into four categories: (1) transfer economies, (2) economies of scale internal to a firm or plant, (3) economies of scale external to a plant but internal to an industry, and (4) economies of scale external even to an industry but present in large multi-industry population concentrations. Although agglomeration economies are generally treated as a separate factor (in part because we know that they exist, but they are hard to measure), we will see that they are closely related to transport costs and labor costs. *Transfer economies,* the first category of agglomeration economies, are in fact the savings in transportation cost to each firm that comes from locating adjacent to others. To the extent that one plant sells a large proportion of its output to a second plant, the location of the first near the second will reduce the delivered price to the second, assure a market for the first, and, ultimately, make the second more competitive in its sale of its products or services. Transfer economies also occur when the products are not delivered by the producer but must be picked up by the purchaser. The convenience of shopping centers is largely related to the travel time saved by shoppers who can perform a variety of purchasing tasks without traveling far between stores. (The characteristically higher prices of products in large, successful shopping centers merely reflects the fact that not all of the benefits of the transfer economies actually accrue to those who shop there. Some benefits accrue as higher profits to store owners, some as high rents for landlords.)

Economies of scale internal to the firm are precisely the scale economies due to specialization that gave rise to our illustrative community above. They are economies of scale that individual firms, even in isolation, are capable of internalizing or gaining the benefits from. They lead to the concentration of population around the plant. *Economies of scale external to a plant but internal to an industry* are reductions in the cost per unit of output to a plant that occur as two or more plants in the same industry expand at a particular place. These external economies of scale arise for a variety of reasons. The presence of several plants in an industry may encourage the development of specialized service industries that provide inputs into the production process more efficiently than that input could be produced in any single plant. The specialized tool-and-die industry that serves several automobile manufacturers in Detroit or the specialized printing industry that serves various advertising firms in New York are examples of services produced at costs below that which the individual firms served could reproduce for themselves. Finally, *economies of scale that are external to both single plants in isolation or even to multiplant industries, but which do occur when many industries grow in one place,* are called *urbanization* economies. Urbanization economies include the availability of improved transportation services such as terminal facilities, a larger and more flexible labor market, commercial and financial services, and more efficient public services. All these may cause the average costs of a firm to fall for the same rate of production if it locates in a larger rather than a smaller community, or in any community rather than in rural areas.

The magnitude of agglomeration economies is difficult to measure for several reasons. First, the production cost data necessary to compare, for example, costs of producing specific products under different conditions of agglomeration tend to be closely guarded competitive secrets of the firms involved. Plants tend to produce not a single product but a whole product line. To find plants using precisely the same technology to produce the same complete product lines in different areas creates a severe sampling problem. And variation across regions for other reasons in the shipping and labor costs make it very difficult to isolate cost differences attributable to specific forms of agglomeration economies.

Raymond Vernon has attempted to grapple with this problem and to identify "external economy industries" (Vernon 1960). He considers them to be "industries producing unstandardized goods, continually changing their process and product, and assiduously avoiding commitments in machinery, buildings, and other fixed capital" (p. 63). His definition, drawn from New York experience, may be problematical. For the situation in New York is one where neither transport costs nor labor costs are advantageous and the continued presence of many industries, he suggests, must mean they are drawn by external economies. Therefore, those industries not otherwise explicable in New York are "external economy industries." But Vernon's description of the nature of these industries and the links that bind them to one-another and collectively to New York is convincing. Vernon found two factors that tended to produce a pronounced clustering of these industries in the New York region: "the life-or-death need of the shops and plants to share certain common facilities, and their need to tap these facilities at top speed." This again, appears to be a function of the specialization of the city in industries that cater to rapidly changing type and quantity of demand. Whether that is generalizable to the agglomeration economies of a Gary, Indiana, petroleum-steel complex is doubtful.

The presence of natural resources or proximity to other raw materials such as raw lumber or specific agricultural products gives rise to a raw materials orientation for some industry. This orientation, again, arises under special conditions with respect to labor and transport costs. When the costs of transporting finished products are substantially lower than the costs of shipping raw materials (as in a production processes such as one refining or lumber milling where raw materials lose considerable weight), processing firms are likely to be led to locate near the sources of raw materials. Labor cost differentials, if any, must be compensated by differences in those shipping costs.

Firms locate, relocate, or expand in places partly on the basis of the cost considerations discussed above and their individual and collective impact upon the costs at which products can be supplied. Success of the firm depends, however, not on supply considerations alone but also on the demand for its products or services. The location factors related to demand are generally summarized under the concept of market size or market potential. The magnitude of the market in an area is always a concern, but the size of the market will not always influence plant location so that the final decision is dominated by market orientation.

Orientation to markets is the fourth general location orientation found in most location theory. Firms tend to be *oriented to markets* when costs of transporting final products are greater than transport costs of assembling the inputs, assuming that labor costs are similar at alternative locations. If labor costs are less away from markets, the transport costs of finished products must be greater than those of gathering inputs by enough to offset the labor cost differences. Market orientation is determined not only by relative labor and transport costs but also by the size and concentration of markets. The size of markets depends upon both the number of people within feasible market areas and the income level of those persons. It is not accidental that one finds little manufacturing of any sort in sparsely populated areas. Areas of concentrated high-income population, on the other hand, tend to generate attraction for industry just by virtue of the markets they represent. New industry locates, the market expands, additional industry is attracted. This is an additional dimension of the cumulative growth process described by Pred.

Relative Importance of the Location Factors

There have been a large number of studies of industrial location patterns and their determinants in recent years. Many of them were designed to study location patterns in specific small areas, and these we omit. One of the first of the more comprehensive studies was done by Glenn McLaughlin and Stefan Robock with respect to plant locations in thirteen southern states (McLaughlin and Robock 1949). They used an interview technique to determine the principal considerations actually used by the managers of eighty-eight plants established in the South after 1945. They found that businessmen frequently employ a two-step procedure: First, they select a general region (perhaps several states), and then they choose a site within the region.

Proximity to markets was easily the leading determinant of location for their sample of plants. Forty-five percent of the plants and more than fifty percent of the employment created was market-oriented. These plants tended to consist of expansions of preexisting firms from other parts of the country that were trying to expand into the southern area.

Proximity to raw materials was the second most important determinant; thirty percent of their plants appeared to be oriented to either perishable or otherwise immobile raw materials or to relatively high raw materials transport costs (e.g., for pulpwood). Labor costs were the third most important determinant; about twenty-five percent of the plants were clearly drawn by the low wages, low unionization, and available surplus labor of the region. For many of these firms, McLaughlin and Robock reported, transportation costs were a small part of the delivered cost of the products.

Wilbur R. Thompson and John M. Mattila conducted a pioneering econometric analysis of postwar state industrial development that included indirect analysis of the relative importance of the various location factors. Working with employment data for twenty two-digit SIC manufacturing industries in each of forty-eight states for each year from 1947 to 1954, they calculated correlation coefficients for absolute growth of employment in each industry and variables reflecting the major hypothetical determinants. They found that growth of the local market, as measured by population growth and personal income growth, accounted for some forty-three to forty-five percent of the variation in state growth rates for all industries. Individual industries tended to show generally lower correlations. The market orientation, somewhat surprisingly, appeared stronger for durable goods industries than for nondurables. They hypothesized, but did not test, that nondurables tended to be more resource-oriented.

Thompson and Mattila found that prior industrialization, as measured by prior increases in manufacturing employment, 1947 investment in manufacturing plant and equipment, and the issuance of patents, were separately capable of explaining from thirty-five percent to thirty-eight percent of interstate variations in growth over the 1947–54 period. They viewed these variables as an early proxy for agglomeration economies of various sorts. They also found that labor market characteristics, that is, average hourly earnings and trade union membership, accounted for only fourteen percent to sixteen percent of the variation. Correlations for specific industries suggested that high wages and strong unions did, in fact, lead to slower growth for some states over that period. The unionization impact, however, was not uniform across industries. Unionization tended to repel about half the foot-loose, lower-skilled nondurable goods industries, while the less mobile, skill demanding durables appeared to thrive in highly unionized labor markets.

An important dimension of market attraction that Thompson and Mattila were able to sort out in their analyses of relative growth rates of employment was the relative effects of income and population. They found that, although increases in both population and personal income were significant correlates of manufacturing employment growth, increases in personal income were considerably more important than population changes. This evidence will be important to the argument that growth in population is not a necessary prerequisite for growth in manufacturing employment. To the extent that income increases can be achieved by upgrading the quality of jobs, welfare increases may occur without population increases.

The classic study by Harvey S. Perloff, Edgar S. Dunn, Jr., Eric E. Lampard, and Richard F. Muth (1960), which is discussed in considerable detail in the following chapter, also contained evidence on industrial location trends. Perloff et al. concluded, after exhaustive treatment of shifts in major industries among major regions and states and over varying long periods, that industry has shifted, over the years, from resource to market orientation. They then placed agglomeration economies as the second most important determinant. But they encountered difficulty in separating market forces from agglomeration forces in their simple correlation analysis. Resource or materials orientation, they suggested, is weakening as products tend to be processed more and as the majority of manufacturing thus becomes further removed from the location of resources.

The most comprehensive and systematic recent attempt to evaluate relative location factors is that of Leonard F. Wheat (1973). He has sought to analyze the relative effects of market size, agglomeration, generalized "urban attraction" (which does not appear distinguishable from markets or agglomeration economies), labor, natural resources, and climate. He used data from the forty-eight contiguous states over the period 1947 to 1963 to derive three growth variables to be analyzed: absolute, per capita, and percentage growth in manufacturing employment. He then employed simple correlation, partial correlation, and multiple correlation techniques to determine relative significance. His findings "leave no doubt that markets and climate are far ahead as the leading influences affecting manufacturing growth in the United States. Labor and thresholds follow as secondary influences. Resources and the urban attraction might best be labeled tertiary influences, although one could easily quarrel about where resources belongs" (p. 183). "Agglomeration," he found, "has no measurable effect on . . . growth."

This conclusion with respect to agglomeration economies appears to be based upon a very narrow definition of the concept. Wheat asserted that agglomeration is the opposite of markets in the sense that the market hypothesis calls for faster growth in the least industrialized states but the agglomeration hypothesis calls for faster growth in the most industrialized ones. Consistent with this interpretation he evaluates the presence of agglomerative forces solely in terms of dummy variables (zero or one) for the more industrialized states and dummy variables for arbitrary prior levels of industrialization (e.g., industrial employment in a state greater than 145,000 or industrial value added greater than $1 billion). He omits, however, the possibility that rapidly growing states will generate new agglomeration economies through industrial growth without surpassing his arbitrary levels.

Wheat also found that "virtually all of the variation in regional growth can be accounted for by *regional* influences. This means that *local* influences merely direct growth to particular cities within preselected regions" (p. 211). This last conclusion carries significant implications for regional development policy, including that pertinent to individual cities, for it further highlights the competition among cities for growth, and it implies that urban growth in a declining region is likely to be almost entirely at the cost of other cities within that region.

The influence of agglomeration economies on industrial location have been analyzed most thoroughly in a recent unpublished study by William R. Latham (1973). Amplifying and extending the previous work of Charles E. Richter (1968, 1969) and M. E. Streit (1969), Latham developed a data base for employment in 199 four-digit SIC manufacturing industries in each of 377 SMSA (Standard Metropolitan Statistical Areas) and non-SMSA personal income regions (as defined by the Bureau of Economic Analysis) that completely cover the United States for the year 1963. From the 1963 national input-output study, he derived measures of supply and demand linkage between each pair of industries as a basis for potential agglomeration economies. Then he analyzed the actual spatial agglomerations of industries, as of 1963, to determine whether agglomerative economies appear to be influential.

He found, first, that there was little evidence of "random" or "footloose" location in any of his industries. The spatial configurations of individual industries suggested that twenty-six percent were notably oriented to labor costs, eighteen percent to final markets, and fourteen percent to raw materials according to his criteria. Significant locational association potentially related to agglomerative linkages were found to be significant for about five percent of the industries. Regression analysis on a random subsample of twenty industries suggested that simple agglomeration economies related to shipping costs between plants were significant determinants of location for more than half, and generalized agglomeration economies were significant determinants for all twenty industries in the subsample. These generalized agglomeration economies may well overlap with market orientation factors, but they suggest rather clearly that the size of an industrial complex or of the industrial component of an economic structure is important for future development.

There is a discouraging lack of information on the locational characteristics of service industries. This is clearly attributable, in part, to the weakness of national and local area statistics on the services. But it may also reflect a bias toward manufacturing industry as the principal source of growth impetus. That such a bias is outmoded may be seen in our earlier discussions of service industries as the principal source of new urban employment. It may be that each industrial job creates a demand for services that increases service employment by more than one job. In that case manufacturing growth, as we will see in the next chapter, may still be the principal growth source. On the other hand, we also know that many services, such as finance, insurance, and large-scale wholesaling are export industries in every sense that manufacturing industries may be. The dearth of research into the location of these exportable services is a major liability in the planning of urban economic development.

Is There a Basic Economic Structure That All Cities Should Have?

Given all of the location tendencies of industry, the related growth and decline of cities, and the resulting economic structures, is there a typical or average or meaningful "target" economic structure toward which cities have evolved or toward which policy should be directed. At first glance the answer would seem to be no. The locational characteristics of virtually every city would seem to be unique, and the economic structure derived from those characteristics would also seem unique to each city. There exists, however, a rather substantial body of research on the patterns of industrial composition that, if read closely, appears to suggest that every city should have certain minimum proportions of its labor force in each industry.

The first study in this vein was that of Gunnar Alexandersson (1956). His work was expanded by Irving Morrissett (1958). The approach was generalized by Edward L. Ullman and Michael F. Dacey (1960) and updated by Ullman, Dacey, and Harold Brodsky (1969).

Alexandersson set out to provide detailed descriptions, including maps, of the distribution of individual industries across cities. His initial purpose was clearly descriptive, but he suggested that such an approach would be useful to the planner in small areas who "often feels a need for comparison with other areas" (p. 10). He attempted to differentiate among cities on the basis of the extent to which certain industries were present in excess of the minimum size necessary to supply the cities' own populations with goods and services of the type that are produced in every "normal" city. He created cumulative distribution diagrams (which relate the percent of gainfully employed population in an industry to the percent of cities that contained such a percent or less) and chose arbitrary points on that diagram to represent the minimum that a city should have. Using the value associated with five percent of the 864 cities surveyed and considering thirty-six different industries, he found proportions that ranged from zero (for manufacturing industries especially) to eight percent of the labor force for "other retail trade" for the minimum that should be found. The variation among cities around these minimum local requirements was considerable, and Alexandersson suggested that cities should limit their comparison to cities of "similar industrial structures." If, however, the purpose of the comparison is to determine whether the distribution of employment is somehow appropriate, the search for other similar cities with which to compare would seem contradictory.

Alexandersson also provided detailed descriptions of the distribution across the United States of each of his thirty-six industries. These industry analyses are not relevant to the question that we are asking here, but they may be useful to planners who are conducting preliminary studies of the feasibility of attracting or expanding a given industry.

The approach was broadened, both in detail and in application, by Irving Morrissett (1958). Morrissett investigated the variation across city size in the proportions of employment in the same set of industries. He found that in almost every industry the minimum local requirements increase with city size. This he interpreted to mean that smaller cities tend to rely upon larger cities for the supply of more of their goods and services and that larger cities are more self-sufficient in that sense. Morrissett also calculated other points on the distribution (other than Alexandersson's fifth percentile, that is) and found that industries vary not only in the proportion associated with the fifth percentile of the cumulative distribution but also in the proportions at other points on the distribution. There appears to be no systematic variation across industries and city size in the relative proportions that should be found of each industry, according to Morrissett's results; but Morrissett apparently failed to note that the results seriously weaken the usefulness of the approach. He hypothesized, instead, that as cities of a particular size class grow, their economic structures should change to conform to the typical structures of the size class into which they move. For such to be true, however, one must assume that the distribution of industries is not changing, that the locational forces are not changing, and that each city corresponds to the average structure with which Morrissett is working. But we know that the spatial pattern of industrial location has been changing substantially, that changes in technology are changing the relative importance of the various location factors, and that variation around the average structure is very great. The likely usefulness of the approach, therefore, seems greatly impaired.

The arbitrariness of choosing any specific point on the cumulative distribution as a basis for asserting minimum requirements was remedied to some extent by the two best-known studies in this area. Edward L. Ullman and Michael F. Dacey (1960) attempted to determine the minimum proportions across city size classes by means of linear regression analysis. They chose the smallest percent found in each city size class for each of only fourteen industry groups and estimated the regression line that would link that to population size. They provided no information on the amount of variation around those regression lines or whether, as would be suggested by Morrissett's analysis, curvilinear estimates were tried. They drew the strongest inferences from their analysis of any of the researchers in the area. Given the regression lines for each industry, they suggested, one could simply read off the "proper" minima for any size city (p. 98). They also showed, counter to their own conclusion, that when cities are divided into groups according to criteria other than size the individual industry minima and the sum over all industries vary significantly.

In a subsequent study, Ullman, Dacey, and Brodsky (1969) updated the earlier study and published estimates of the excess employment over the size-specific minimum requirements for each of 101 SMSAs in 1960. They then derived indices of specialization from these estimates, under the assumption that the relative concentration of excesses over their predetermined minima was a relevant measure of specialization.

The minimum requirements approach to basic economic structure has been criticized widely by Richard T. Pratt (1968) and Sven Ilberis (1964) because the specified minimum depends upon the number of industries with which one wishes to work. This does not merely mean that as you break one industry into two components the minima in the two add to the previous minimum for the single group. Rather, the greater the degree of disaggregation, the lower the sum of the minima across all industries, even though one is merely treating the same economic phenomena with greater detail.

A more serious criticism might be levied against the very concept itself. There is no reason to expect every city to have any employment in any industry that possesses a market area larger than the average city. Only those industries for which market areas are very small, that is, no larger than the smallest city in the set of cities one is studying, may reasonably be expected to have some employment in every city. No one would seriously assert that we could expect to find a certain nonzero proportion of employees engaged in aircraft fabrication in every city! Is there any increase in insight if we dissolve the focus and look at the more general transport equipment category, or, as Ullman, Dacey, and Brodsky propose—all durable manufacturing?

The proportion of employment that any urban area should have in each category will depend upon its locational characteristics, human and physical capital, development history, and the conditions prevailing in the regional, national, and international economies. One can assert that a greater proportion should be in one industry rather than another only if one can demonstrate that the long-term income level or other qualitative welfare characteristics of the local economy would be improved by such a change in structure.

If one must find a basis for comparison, forgetting the uniqueness of every city's situation, it is more reasonable to turn to average proportions employed in each sector for cities of comparable size than to base the

Table 2-1

Proportion of Employment in Each Industry by Size-of-Place Category (U.S. National Averages, 1960)

Industry	Nonmetro Counties	Metropolitan Areas Population		
		50,001 to 200,000	200,001 to 1,600,000	1,600,000 or more
Primary	20.7	7.1	3.4	1.0
Construction	6.3	6.0	6.1	4.8
Manufacturing	21.0	25.1	27.5	30.2
Utilities	1.3	1.4	1.4	1.3
Mainly business services	10.5	13.4	16.4	18.7
Transportation	3.4	3.9	4.4	4.6
Communications	0.9	1.2	1.3	1.5
Wholesale	2.3	3.0	3.8	3.9
Finance, insurance, real estate	2.2	3.3	4.5	5.6
Business/repair	1.8	2.1	2.5	3.1
Mainly consumer services	31.5	34.8	32.8	31.7
Retail	14.3	15.0	14.8	13.9
Recreation/entertainment	3.2	4.0	3.8	3.9
Private household	3.5	3.4	2.8	2.2
Medical/education	10.4	12.4	11.5	11.7
Government	6.2	9.0	8.4	7.0
Administration	3.8	4.5	5.2	5.5
Armed forces	2.4	4.5	3.2	1.5
Industry not reported	2.6	3.1	4.1	5.3
Total	100.0	100.0	100.0	100.0

Source: Adapted from Thomas M. Stanback, Jr. and Richard V. Knight, *The Metropolitan Economy, The Process of Employment Expansion* (New York: Columbia University Press, 1970), Table 4-3, p. 81.

comparison on expected minimum levels. The median data calculated by Morrissett, but not reported, would serve such a purpose. Thomas M. Stanback Jr. and Richard V. Knight (1970) have calculated mean industrial structures for three ranges of size and for nonmetropolitan counties for 1960. Their data, reproducd in Table 2-1, provide a broad basis for comparison; but they should not be interpreted as meaningful goals toward which any urban economy ought to be restructured.

Conclusions

We have examined the origins of urban economic structures over a range of dimensions, from the broadest characteristics of the city as part of an urban economic system to the individual factors considered by firms when they decide to locate a new plant. We have moved from a simple illustrative model of the economic founding of a town to evaluation of available descriptions of the economic structures of the nation's largest cities. It would seem that we can draw several conclusions from this survey of the origin and determinants of urban economic structures. First, the position of every urban economy within the national economy and the intricate relationship that its economic structure has to the economic structure of other urban places in its region both suggest that the amount of leverage that residents in any single city have over their own economic structure is severely limited. National economic development has, until recently, favored the growth and development of older, established large cities. The present trend, however, appears to be one that favors on many levels both small cities in the shadow of the metropolises and newer cities distant from the traditional urban centers. Decentralization of previously heavily concentrated industries implies problems of adaptation for previously favored cities (if the presence of some of these industries can be considered, on balance, a "favor"). The increasing orientation of industry to markets may provide a mitigating effect, for the large traditional cities will continue to provide the greatest concentrated markets in the nation.

The final conclusion that appears to emerge readily from the analysis of the determinants of economic structure is that generalizations are difficult to make and that the application of generalizations to individual cities may be very hazardous. The development history of the economic structure of every city has been unique. No two cities have ever enjoyed precisely the same historical relationship to national or regional growth. No two cities have ever had precisely the same sets of locational influences over time. The design of an urban economic development plan must, then, be a one-of-a-kind enterprise. Even if two cities had complete agreement on development goals (a difficult task, as we shall see), the necessary development policies are likely to be different. Different industries will be appropriate, different incentive programs may be required, and different paths to the achievement of the goals are probable. This conclusion reduces to the requirement that planners in each urban area know not only the composition of the economic structure at the present, but also the historical pattern of development, the historical factors affecting that development, the contemporary relative advantages of the area within the regional and national context, and the prospects for expansion of the specific local component of each national industry represented locally. These requirements also serve to illuminate the minimal usefulness of many mechanistic economic base studies that merely project for a region its share of existing national industries without determining the specific reasons for expansion or contraction of local components. The development of such an understanding is not an easy task, nor is it one that is likely to be inexpensive. But if the burden of evidence on the determinants of economic structure leads toward any simple conclusion, it is that the unique elements of each city's development history retain significant influence over the past and future development of each city. It is these differentiating unique elements that must be known if the common elements are to be interpreted accurately. And it is these unique elements that may provide the most effective basis for an urban economic development program.

3

What Determines the Level of Income in Urban Areas?

There is probably no measure of economic welfare that synopsizes the economic aspirations of individuals more fully than their relative level of real income. Income levels are far from perfect measures of human satisfaction, for they fail to reflect many social and cultural dimensions of individual satisfaction. But to the extent that they do reflect the relative ability of individuals to meet basic material needs and to acquire material goods above basic needs, relative income levels represent necessary but not sufficient conditions for personal satisfaction for most persons.

It is important to note three aspects of income measures as applied to cities. First, it is more likely the relative income among cities rather than any absolute income level that will be of policy concern. For it is the "invidious" comparison of income levels that is likely to spur lower-income cities to instigate urban development programs. The variation in overall income levels across cities is not, on average, so great that many city governments are likely to encounter unacceptable average absolute income levels. The levels achieved in other communities may be taken as measures of what is possible within the national and regional economy, and it is those levels that appear as implicit targets. Second, average income levels across cities mask variations within cities in the distribution of income. A city with a given level of income that is distributed relatively equitably is less likely to encounter dissatisfaction than one in which that same average level consists of a small proportion of the population with very high income and a large proportion with very low. We discuss these and other dimensions of income inequality in urban development in Chapter 5. High wages paid sporadically in heavily fluctuating employment produce levels of economic welfare considerably below those associated with similar wages paid regularly. Large variations from year to year in income levels in a city have important welfare implications over the longer term. Since most analyses of urban income have used measures of income in a specific single year, instability is another dimension not generally encompassed in analyses of relative average income levels. The analysis of instability is the subject of Chapter 4.

Neither growth in population nor growth in the quantity of goods produced in a city nor, for that matter, increases in the number of jobs available will necessarily increase the level of income in that city. What, then, does determine that one city has relatively high real income and another relatively low? There are no simple answers; but in this chapter we attempt to sort out the various dimensions of the urban economic structure that, when combined in the simultaneous general equilibrium relations discussed in the previous chapter, determine the level of affluence of any specific city. We also consider the evidence available on the characteristics of cities that appear to be developing more rapidly as measured by increases in real income levels. The focus is twofold: (1) What is known about the determinants of urban affluence, and (2) what does that imply with respect to policies for increasing urban income levels?

It is appropriate to recall that the demographic and educational characteristics of the population of different cities have considerable influence over the average income levels that they will have. There are fairly clear patterns of relationship, for example, between age and income levels for individuals within a specific occupation. Although peak earnings occur at somewhat different ages in different occupations, it is generally true that the incomes of persons from ages forty to fifty-five are higher than those of persons from ages twenty to thirty or of persons aged sixty-five and above. Cities that have a population with an unusual age distribution should expect to have an income level which reflects that to some extent. It would be inappropriate, for example, to expect that cities with relatively high proportions of their populations composed of retired elderly, such as St. Petersburg or Tucson, should have average income levels as high as otherwise comparable cities with more typical age distributions.

In much the same way the educational and vocational background of the labor force in a city could serve as a barrier to relatively high income levels. Salaries and wages tend to be associated with worker productivity in such a manner that cities with labor forces that are relatively less skilled or less educated should not expect average incomes comparable to those of cities where the quality of the human resources is in some senses greater.

Data on relative income levels is not reported in a form that has been adjusted for such demographic or educational differences in the basis for expected income, and an argument could be made for suggesting that in the latter case the adjustment would be inappropriate. That is, low educational skill levels are a proper object of urban development policy, so one should not ignore such differences among cities as is implicit in adjusting them away. Demographic characteristics related to the age structure, however, are less likely to be an object of development policy. Failure to adjust for them forces unrealistic goals upon development policy.

Our survey and evaluation of the literature proceeds in three steps. First, we review the various theoretical approaches that have been offered in recent years to explain relative urban income levels. This literature has tended to stress employment changes and income changes separately, so we then review studies of the changing employment structure of regions within the United States and the relationship of those changes to relative income levels. Finally, we review those studies that have been oriented specifically to the growth of regional and urban income levels.

The total income earned by any individual may be divided into three components: (1) wages, salaries, or proprietory income; (2) property income, including profits, interest, and rents; and (3) transfer payments from other individuals (e.g., alimony) or from the government (e.g., social security payments). Wages, salaries, and the equivalent income of proprietors constitute more than eighty percent of income for most individuals (Perloff, et al. 1960, p. 494). Property income does not generally require the physical presence of the person earning it. Rents, profits, interest, and dividends may accrue to persons residing far from the property or the institution in which they are generated. Transfer payments tend to be established by political decisions that are not necessarily coincident with the market forces that govern most of the rest of the economy. In that which follows, we shall emphasize the economic, geographical, and political determinants of levels of wages, salaries, and proprietary income. These three sources are frequently combined as participation income since they relate to the income received for participating in local labor markets.

The Export-base Approach to Levels and Growth of Urban Income

The most venerable tool in the urban planners economic toolkit over the past twenty-five years has been what is alternatively called the economic base or export base or export multiplier model. Formalization of the approach tends to be associated with Charles M. Tiebout (1956, 1962) and Richard B. Andrews (1953, 1956). The economic model or approach to urban income analysis given this name has evolved from the initial empirical recognition that a significant portion of the production of urban areas is sold in markets that are outside the city itself. To the extent that such markets are as important for early city formation and as subsequent determinants of growth as our illustrative example in the previous chapter suggested, an orientation to urban growth that analyzes these markets appears to be a logical starting place. The *export-base approach* refers in general to all those frameworks that relate urban income, employment, and production directly to the exports of the area.

The export-base approach does not deny that some firms within a city produce for local consumption. Rather, it suggests that the demand for locally produced goods and services is not really determined within the city; it is determined indirectly by the amount of labor employed and the amount of income generated in producing the city's exports of goods and services. Although it may appear easy to separate conceptually the local production from the export production, it is in reality very difficult. The production of steel that is shipped to another city is fairly clearly export production. Teaching in a locally oriented primary school appears clearly to be local production. But what about local production of steel that is shipped to a local plant and manufactured into the pickup truck used by the steel worker to get to his job? The truck was sold in a local market but is being used by a worker whose primary occupation is export-oriented. What proportion of the truck or the original steel is an indirect export and what proportion clearly local production? The actual measurement problems are even more difficult.[a]

In terms of employment the simplest form of export base asserts that there exists a stable relationship between an area's total employment and the number of jobs in the export sector. That is, a certain number of jobs in the local sector are viewed as supported by or associated with each job in the export sector. Then, total employment increases will be led by increases in employment in the export sector due largely to factors beyond or external to the control of local producers. The magnitude of total increases in employment that corresponds to increases in export employment will be some multiple of the export employment increase, for the new export employment is assumed to generate additional income that will be spent locally and increase demand for local services.

The relationship between increases in export employment and increases in total employment is assumed to be stable. Based on this stability an employment multiplier is then applied, rather mechanically, to any expected increases in export employment in order to determine changes in total employment. Unfortunately, the employment multiplier has been repeatedly shown to be unstable. Estimates of growth that use it are subject to very large margins of error.

The export-base model has also been specified for the analysis of growth in income. The conceptual basis is identical. Income is derived by some local residents from the production of goods for export. That part of their income that they then spend for locally produced goods and services determines the amount of income available for persons working in the production of local goods and services. The economic-base multiplier in this case is defined as the ratio of the area's total income to the income earned in the export sector. The larger the multiplier, the larger is the

---

[a] For discussions of the alternative techniques that have evolved to resolve these problems see Ralph W. Pfouts (1960).

sensitivity of the local economy to changes in economic conditions in its external markets. Sophisticated versions of the export-base approach incorporate different multipliers for each major export industry, based upon the amount of income generated in it, public and private investment, and detailed linkages between industries within the region and industries outside the region. No matter how finely individual industries are broken out, all export-base models share a common set of rather severe problems.

Criticisms of the Export-base Approach

The export-base approach is built upon a series of relatively harsh assumptions. It is assumed, for example, that income and employment in a city are not changed by any influences other than changes in the level of exports, that the amount of income spent for local products is stable over wide ranges of income change and relatively long periods, and that the amount of income generated locally by each dollar spent locally is also unchanging. But, as cities grow in both population and income, new local services tend to be provided so that the imports of the area are reduced and the multiplier rises without direct relationship to exports.

The approach also assumes that there are no changes in any of the prices of inputs or products that determined the magnitude of the multiplier at the time it was calculated, and that all the additional labor and capital required to expand production will be available immediately and without an increase in wages or rates of profit. The price and wage instability of the 1970s makes such assumptions particularly hazardous.

The strongest bases for criticism yet remain, for export-base analysis neglects to specify the internal mechanisms that are at work in any area's economy. It uses the industrial structure at one point in time to predict the industrial structure over a number of years into the future without recognizing or considering the determinants of the evolution of that structure, the direction it was evolving, or the likely significance of those determinants for future evolution of the urban economy.

As summarized by Werner Z. Hirsch (1973):

The assumptions implicit in the export-base framework are quite unrealistic, so that it conveys very little about the behavior of decision units or the economic processes within the urban economy. At best, the framework permits the approximation of levels of economic activity over the short run, during which the distribution of income, the industry mix, and the production techniques used in the urban area are not subject to substantial change [p. 194].

The Labor-supply Approach to Levels and Growth of Urban Income

Export-base analysis, as noted above, developed out of the practical experience of planners and as a response to their pragmatic needs for estimates of urban growth based on readily available data and capable of relatively simple explanation. A second approach to the problem of explaining and predicting relative income areas among regions (including urban areas) in a large open economy has been derived from more deductive theoretical reasoning as an extension of theoretical international trade models and national economic growth models. This more theoretical approach is called by economists the neoclassical model of regional growth for it stems from a large set of models that emphasize the supply of potential factors of production and that assume, as the classical economists tended to assume, that the simple availability of factors of production would assure their use in the production of *something*. The regional and urban variant of the neoclassical growth models tend to focus most heavily on the availability of labor for reasons that are noted below. For that reason and to distinguish them in more parallel fashion from the export-base models discussed above, we refer to neoclassical models here as labor-supply models of urban growth. In general, just as the export-base models assumed that all the necessary capital and labor would be available when needed to expand production as external demand increased, the labor-supply approach tends to assume that demand for regional products is of minor concern and that relative supplies of labor and capital determine regional output and income.

George H. Borts and Jerome L. Stein have presented the most thorough explanation of the labor-supply approach and have applied it to the analysis of interstate differentials in per capita income levels and growth (Borts and Stein 1964). Richard F. Muth has produced an important theoretical and empirical application of essentially the same approach to the analysis of differential growth in employment and income among large United States cities (Muth 1969). Muth's empirical analysis suggests, as we shall see, that on several key points the labor-supply approach appears to be superior to the export-base approach for explaining relative growth. Horst Siebert, finally, has offered an approach that synthesizes some of each of the "camps" (though still clearly leaning toward the neoclassical orientation). Siebert combined analysis of the demand for regional products and the supply of regional inputs to determine total production and income levels. He then derived a lengthy series of theorems on differential growth that remain empirically unverified but that, nonetheless, offer an intriguing basis for examining alternative urban development policies.

The labor-supply model of growth in total regional production, as presented by Borts and Stein, is based upon an assumed simplified economy in which government policy (not incorporated in the model) or long-term trends in the economy maintain full employment. Growth in output can come from one of three sources: (1) an increase in the quantity of capital and labor resources, (2) technological change that makes either labor or capital more productive than it had been previously, or (3) re-allocation of capital and labor resources from less productive to more productive industries. When the model is applied to the analysis of rela-tive growth in two or more regions, it is assumed that prices for export products and for capital goods are set in competitive national markets and are essentially the same for producers in all regions. Production processes are assumed to be the same in all regions, and there are no economies of scale. Under these conditions Borts and Stein have shown algebraically that the wage level will be determined by the ratio of capital to labor. That is, not surprisingly, that the greater the amount of capital per laborer in a region, the higher the wage level. Over the long run, they then suggest, if capital and labor are mobile, there should be a tendency toward equalization of wage levels across all regions. The owners of capital will make higher profits in low-wage areas and will be induced to move there. Wage earners will obtain higher incomes in high-wage areas and should tend to move there. The loss of capital and the increase in labor in high-wage areas should tend to reduce wages there. The loss of labor and the addition of capital in low-wage areas should tend to raise wages there.

When confronted with the fact that in two of three periods studied the quantity of capital grew more rapidly in high-wage areas than in low-wage areas, they show that this may well be related to the rates at which the available labor force expands. Since the labor supply for any particular industry can come from only three sources (barring previous unemploy-ment)—(1) new entrants into the labor force, (2) migration, and (3) movement from other industries—they hypothesize that increases in man-ufacturing employment should be most rapid in those areas where wages are low and where the smaller proportions of the labor force are already in manufacturing. To the extent that expanding industries offer higher wages than industries previously in an area (as they must if they wish to recruit labor), per capita income should rise most rapidly in those same areas. To the extent that the increased labor needs are met by in-migration of new labor force, the ratio of capital to labor will rise less rapidly, and wages and incomes will rise less rapidly.

This is an important conclusion for the economic development of cities. Growth in the value of output requires both additional capital and the labor force to work with it. Urban and regional economies may grow at very rapid rates, in terms of output, employment, and population *without* increases in the average level of income if migration brings in new labor force from lower wage jobs elsewhere. Urban *development* will be associated with growth in output produced only if the rate of increase in capital (new plants) creates jobs that pay higher than average wages at a rate in excess of the rate at which migrants are attracted to an area. For any given rate of increase in available local capital (or new job creation), the more rapid the growth of the population of an urban area, the slower the rate of growth of income and the slower the rate at which the urban economy develops in this sense.

Muth extended the study by Borts and Stein by formulating a model of urban growth, on neoclassical bases, which assumed that growth in employment and migration are determined simultaneously, rather than separately or sequentially. This relationship is important if one is to explain the failure of capital movements and labor migration to eliminate the wage and income differentials among cities. Muth formulated an algebraic model to determine the effect of employment increases upon migration and the effects of migration upon employment increases in both an export sector and a domestic sector in a hypothetical urban economy.

Muth shows that in the labor-supply model, not only the price of output and capital goods but also the money wage rate is determined outside the export sector by prices in national markets for export products and for capital goods. An increase in demand for export products does not lead to an increase in total employment in the region by some base multiplier, according to Muth. Rather, it merely leads to a shift of labor from local production to export production. Increases in local money wages will be determined by increases in the prices of export products. Increases in total employment, considered automatic by export-base theorists can occur, in Muth's view, only if labor force participation increases, migration occurs, or both.

The implications of Muth's theoretical analysis for urban development policy appears clear (and strangely reminiscent of the policy implications of export-base approaches): Incomes will rise most rapidly in those urban economies that produce products whose prices are rising most rapidly in the national economy or the costs of whose inputs are falling most rapidly in national markets. It is not sufficient to have simple increases in the quantity produced (demand shifts matched by supply shifts). Simple growth in output will not generate higher standards of living for an urban economy.

Horst Siebert has joined strands from both export-base and labor-supply approaches to present an expanded composite model of regional economic growth. He adds specific considerations of technological change, the regional transport system, and regional social institutions into the set of local resources that he suggests determine potential output. Then he introduces migration of labor, movement of capital, and the demand for products in the region as equally important external determinants of actual output and changes in potential output. Working then with a two-region model and the formal system of equations that interrelate actual and potential output, he proposes a series of theorems on why one regional economy grows faster than another. Although they are theorems from the point of view of the deductive mathematical framework within which he was working, we shall consider some of them as hypotheses to be evaluated in the empirical studies that we discuss below. Siebert (1969) formulated his theorems around differential growth in output, assuming that interregional income differences are "the result of dynamic processes of economic growth" based on different prior rates of growth of output (p. 134). By emphasizing income growth, we can reformulate some of his theorems as hypotheses specific to urban development.

Siebert suggests, "Growth differences between regions will be higher, the stronger the differences in the rate of inventions and the lower the mobility of technical knowledge" (p. 135). Whether "participation income" is increased by technological change would depend upon the nature of that change. Labor-saving technological change produces a result equivalent to an increase in the supply of labor, changing the ratio of capital to labor, and reducing wage rates. A comparable hypothesis for regional income would thus be as follows: income growth differences between regions will be higher, the stronger the differences in the rate of capital-augmenting inventions, the lower the mobility of technical knowledge, or the greater the concentration of property income recipients in a given region with labor-augmenting technical change.

Siebert writes, "A growth differential can exist only if differing factor mobilities prevail." To the extent that regional income growth is more closely associated with changing wages than with changing profit rates, differentials in income growth will be greater in the region that gains more capital than labor or in which labor flows out more rapidly than capital.

Siebert adds external economies to the neoclassical model, and concludes, "The more immobile external economies are interregionally, the greater the growth differential." External economies reduce the costs of production in those places where they may be internalized. This applies directly to income.

Finally, Siebert suggests, "A growth differential caused by the immobility of factors may be reinforced or weakened by the movement of commodities [interregional trade]. The reinforcing effect is a function of changes in the terms of "trade" (p. 146). This concurs with Muth's analysis and implies that those regions whose products are rising in price will enjoy the greatest gains in income.

Criticisms of the Labor-supply Model

Harry W. Richardson has leveled a vigorous barrage of criticism at the neoclassical approach (Richardson 1973, p. 69):

> Neoclassical models have dominated regional growth theory much as they have dominated growth theory in general. However, it is even more difficult to justify this domination at the regional level. The background assumptions of neoclassical growth theory are inapplicable to the regional economy. For instance, the full employment assumption is not usually relevant to regional economics since to a marked extent regional problems emerge because of substantial inter-regional differences in the degree of resource (and particularly labour) utilization. Similarly, perfect competition cannot be assumed in regional economic analysis since space itself and the existence of transport costs limits competition; oligopoly, pure monopoly or monopolistic competition are much more appropriate market structures. Indeed, if we were to adopt neoclassical models in their pure unadulterated form there would be no such field as regional economics.

There is no doubt that the complex reality of the regional economy tends to fit the simplest versions of the Borts and Stein model poorly. But Richardson's inference that proliferation of the approach would spell the end of regional economics may be a bit harsh. Borts and Stein were hard pressed to explain observed behavior with their simple aggregate model, but their formulation, which incorporated adjustment mechanisms, appeared fairly consistent with the pattern of interstate growth in the United States. Richardson appears to have been unaware of Muth's study, and he would have been impressed by Muth's ability to tailor the neoclassical model to an analysis of many of the same processes that export-base analysis attempts to explain. The labor-supply approach does tend to omit phenomena such as agglomeration economies in location and urbanization, differing transport costs, and interdependence of location decisions that we know to be important. But no export-base model comes much closer to these phenomena. In fact, the failure of our conceptual models to incorporate phenomena of such central importance to regional and urban development is a ringing critique of the entire field and a fundamental obstacle to the formulation of urban development policy.

Other Approaches to Urban Economic Development

Stanislaw Czamanski has offered an alternative to export-base models, which he suggests incorporates more of the specific determinants of regional growth. Rather than estimating future growth of an urban area on the basis of a single questionable relationship, the ratio of export to service employment or income, he notes,

> . . . it seems rather useful to view the city not so much as a trading or producing area but rather as a center competing with all other places within the national economy for job-creating investments. In this view, new investments more than present production trends are the important elements in defining the spatial equilibrium between all places within the nation. The variables are then the relative locational advantages and disadvantages of places [1964, p. 177].

The model he proposed was kept simple so that small-area planners working with limited data might be able to use it. He distinguished among three categories of industries: geographically oriented industries, complementary industries, and urban-oriented industries. *Geographically oriented industries* are "industries whose main locational factors are geographical or conditioned by the environment." For example, resource based industries, industries requiring railway junctions, ports, or other transportation facilities are considered geographically oriented because "investments in this category of economic activity do not depend on the size and character of urban development." *Complementary industries* consist of "all enterprises producing services or goods for a limited number of large customers . . . located in the same area." The number and size of complementary industries thus depend directly on the number and size of geographically oriented industries in a city. *Urban-oriented industries* are those "for which the existence of the city is the main locational factor," and their size is assumed to be a direct function of the total size of the city.

The Czamanski approach offers several advantages over export-base models, but it shares serious conceptual problems. It escapes the relatively mechanistic use of the base-ratio by substituting the proportion of geographically oriented industries as the crucial growth parameter. This latter measure does have greater location-theory content, but it is as difficult to define and measure as the export production of the former approach. How can one separate industries in an area, with confidence, to isolate those that are there solely because of the locational advantages of the area? Must they be plants that do not sell locally, either to consumers or to other plants? Are complementary industries only those that sell solely to other local plants?

This approach is important to development planners in small areas, however, for at least two reasons: First, it reiterates the importance of emphasizing the specific locational characteristics of the area and of relating development efforts to them. Second, it demonstrates a simple alternative to the export-base approach that requires little more data and little greater effort.

Wilbur R. Thompson has long proposed the most intuitively appealing pragmatic approaches to urban economic development. His most important theoretical work, *A Preface to Urban Economics* (1965), "broke the surface" for urban development analyses in many places. He sought to offer a set of hypotheses about what determines whether cities will grow and whether, with or without growth, they will accomplish the development goals discussed here.

His approach is heavily oriented to the industrial composition of urban employment. "Simply said," he wrote, "high-wage export industries produce a high-income town. . . ." (p. 2). The high-income town, however, depends upon both the demand for the labor services of its population in such high-wage industries and the determinants of the quantity and quality of the local area resources. He asserts that "the most challenging urban growth theory and the most compelling urban growth problems arise out of interurban competition for growth and the development of the national system of cities" (p. 12). For an individual city, the essence of long-run growth in population or income is "the transition— sometimes orderly, sometimes chaotic—of the local economy from one export base to another as the area matures in what it can do, and as rising per capita income and technological progress change what the national economy wants done."

Thompson has repeatedly suggested that differences in the competitive structures of local industries and differences in competition in the local labor force are significant determinants of the extent to which growth in output is converted into growth in income. The local industrial structure, he contends, combine with skill levels and economic power "the two generic determinants of the level of income," to determine relative income in each area.

Though Thompson associates his analysis with no specific school of economic thought, he nonetheless challenges all students of urban development with a virtually unending stream of hypotheses on the determinants of urban income levels and of their rates of change.

Skill and power combine with industrial structure, for example, in three kinds of industries that he believes will be found associated with high average income levels. First, highly skilled workers in industries producing new products are likely to benefit doubly: High skills imply high productivity and high wages; new products will tend to have monopoly power over markets until competitors develop. Until that period they can well afford high wages; hence, industries with high rates of invention and innovation will provide a continuing basis for high local income.

A second combination of characteristics of high-income industries are those that are highly concentrated, highly specialized, and generally non-competitive for that reason. Again, the market power of such industries, according to Thompson, provides a basis for higher than average wages and, therefore, higher than average income levels in the cities where such firms are located. The simple existence of market power for products, however, does not assure that the higher-than-average profits that such power creates will be passed along to employees as higher wages. The combination of market power and aggressive unions offers even greater likelihood of high wages and high local income, according to Thompson.

If continuous innovation is the key to high incomes in industries that are not highly concentrated and free of competition, then the contributions to that innovation from local services and other local producers may be the key to sustained high incomes. For, as Thompson notes:

> . . . the long range viability of any area must rest ultimately on its capacity to invent and/or innovate or otherwise acquire new export bases.
> The economic base of the larger metropolitan area is, then, the creativity of its universities and research parks, the sophistication of its engineering firms and financial institution, the persuasiveness of its public relations and advertising agencies, the flexibility of its transportation networks and utility systems, and all the other dimensions of infrastructure that facilitate the quick and orderly transfer from old dying bases to new growing ones [1968, p. 53].

Hypotheses on Raising Urban Income Levels

Prior to beginning an analysis of a number of empirical studies of relative regional income levels, employment composition, and changes in both, it may be useful to summarize some of the hypotheses that emerge from the various approaches discussed above. Each approach tended to emphasize one or more critical dimensions of the urban economic structure that presumably should provide the basis for policy aimed at changing levels or rates of growth of per capita income.

From the export-base approach we can derive the hypothesis that those areas which have an industrial structure consisting of fast-growing industries (industries in which either total output or employment is growing rapidly) should be the areas with relatively high rates of growth. The approach also suggests that those areas with high-wage export industries should have higher levels of income.

The labor-supply approach produces different hypotheses. From that approach we are led to believe that areas with a predominance of low-wage, slow-growing industries should enjoy relatively high rates of growth in both income and output as capital moves to take advantage of the low-cost labor force. Income levels should be initially higher in those areas with relative labor scarcity, but migration should gradually diminish the discrepancies. The policy for low-income urban areas implicit in this approach is to seek higher wage industries while simultaneously encouraging out-migration of both excess labor and low-wage industry. The labor-supply approach would also suggest that an urban economy specialized in industry employing the greatest amount of capital per worker (or industries in which value added per worker is high) would tend to have the highest level of income. And those areas whose industries enjoyed the greatest increase in prices or the greatest decreases in nonlabor costs would enjoy the highest rates of income growth.

Czamanski's model is almost too simple to use as a basis for detailed hypotheses, but one can attempt to infer from his approach hypotheses that are generally consistent with it. Czamanski would expect that those areas with greatest locational advantage for their principal geographically oriented industry and areas with the most rapidly expanding geographically oriented industry will grow most rapidly in terms of population. He has not offered an income-determining variant of his model, but it would follow from its basic logic that those geographically oriented industries that produce the highest wages and that are most closely linked to complementary industries with high wages will yield relatively high-income urban areas. Capital-intensive industrial complexes would be consistent with this approach.

Thompson has offered us hypotheses on the competitive, concentrative, innovative, unionized characteristics of industries. He would thus expect to find the highest income levels in traditional centralized manufacturing cities and the highest rate of growth of incomes in those areas associated with continuous introduction of new technology in plants or industries with considerable union influence and in areas with high skill levels.

In the remainder of this chapter, a series of empirical studies of these phenomena are compared and contrasted to determine the extent to which the various hypotheses have been upheld in United States experience.

Relative Growth of Output, Employment, and Income per Capita

If one wishes to analyze the structure and growth of an urban economy, it is equally reasonable to orient oneself to the total value of output from that economy or to total employment levels or to the total income of the area. Or one might be just as interested in the effects of all of the above upon total urban population growth. The literature on urban and regional growth is full of studies of the determinants, the correlates, and the consequences of growth in each of these variables. If, however, one is primarily oriented to the welfare of urban residents, to the interaction between the urban economy and the quality of life, as we are here, then the principal growth to which one will want to be oriented is growth in income per capita.

Data on income per capita are difficult to develop. Models of income per capita are even more scarce. One of the essential dimensions of the urban economy is that it is completely open to the inflow and outflow of migrants. Models of per capita income would require at least three inter-related parts: (1) a model that determines changes in regional output or employment, (2) a model that determines the conversion of output or employment into local income, and (3) a model that, given output or employment and total income, determines the effect of the first two models on the size of the regional population so that per capita income levels may be determined. The Muth model, above, comes closer to that which is needed than any other formulated to date.

If we are to make use of as much of the available literature on urban growth processes as possible, we shall want to consider some studies that have been done using the abundant data on employment composition, employment change, and regional output and income in the aggregate. To do so, we must consider for a moment the pitfalls associated with equating growth in employment with growth in income or, more generally, with increases in the quality of life in a given area. The digression would also be useful in a wider context, for one of the errors frequently seen in ill-conceived urban and regional development programs is the assumption that growth in output or employment will necessarily imply growth in per capita local income.

Harvey S. Perloff et al. have noted that differences in the kind of employment growth are significantly related to population growth and income growth. They found that from 1920 to 1950 population growth by states had a rank correlation with the proportion of state labor force employed in manufacturing of -0.32; total personal income had a coefficient of $+0.09$; and per capita income had $+0.57$. Conversely, for the same period population growth showed a $+0.06$ correlation with agricultural employment; total income showed -0.24; and per capita income -0.48 (1960, p. 98). Per capita income in each case was related to changes in economic structure in the same general way but to a much different degree than total income. In other words, increases in manufacturing employment and decreases in agricultural employment had very different relationships with population, total income, and per capita income.

New jobs will not necessarily raise the quality of life. Thomas M. Stanback, Jr. and Richard V. Knight (1970) have shown that the employment expansion process in metropolitan economies consists of a complex combination of job increases and job decreases. Whether employment expansion will raise per capita income levels depends upon several things: (1) the source of the labor force employed; (2) the wage levels paid in the new employment; (3) the rate of expansion; and (4) the linkages between the new employment and preexisting employment. If the expanded labor force consists solely of new migrants to an area, whether per capita income increases will depend on the remaining three considerations, for if wage-levels are below the previous average, if the native labor force is expanding and if induced employment increases are negligible, per capita income could fall. If some of the new employment absorbed previously unemployed workers or drew some workers from lower wage jobs, then employment increase could raise per capita income even if the wage levels paid were below the previous average or if related employment increases were negligible. The development strategies of seeking new jobs irrespective of wage levels or their relationship to the prior economy appears to be based upon this notion. So long as some local individuals have the opportunity to upgrade their employment status, the reasoning goes, the employment expansion is beneficial to the urban economy. The fallacy of this can be seen in a simple example.

Imagine a city with a population of 100,000, a labor force of 50,000, an average income per employee of $6,000 per year, and consequently per capita income of $3,000 per year. Assume that a large new plant employing 1,000 workers and paying an average of $5,000 per employee per year locates in the city. Let 100 of those new jobs be filled by local workers who upgrade themselves from jobs that had previous average earnings of $4,500 per year, and assume that those very low-wage jobs are lost. Let another 100 jobs be filled by previously unemployed workers and the remainder (800) by new migrants to the city. If those migrants bring families of the same average size as those of previous residents of the city, the situation after the new firm locates will give the city 1,600 new residents, a net increase of $4,550,000 in payrolls ($5,000 × 1,000 − $4,500 × 100), and a resulting per capita income of $2,990 per year. Even with the favorable assumption of hiring ten percent of the new plant from the totally unemployed, per capita income falls. If employment increase is to be considered synonymous with income increase, one must specify the conditions with respect to sources of labor and wage levels.

A similar set of cautions must be raised with respect to assuming that output increases imply increases in per capita income. Simple expansion of output that draws migrants at constant wage rates will not raise income levels. Increases in output that occur less rapidly than increases in the labor force could, all else equal, be associated with falling average income levels. Focus upon the per capita effects is essential!

To What Extent are Income Levels Associated with Industrial Structure?

Empirical analyses of regional income differentials are far less abundant than analyses of regional employment characteristics. Comparable data on income is much less readily available than employment data. Analyses of income differentials across urban areas are virtually nonexistent. Urban area analysis, as discussed earlier, is essentially similar to analysis for any carefully defined region. All along we have been using region and urban area virtually interchangeably. Empirical studies of income differentials using states as the regional basis have been undertaken by a number of authors since 1950. Let us look at some of their results and then qualify them for application to cities.

One of the earliest analyses of the relationship between income and industrial structure was undertaken by Simon Kuznets using census data for 1950 (Kuznets 1958). Kuznets grouped the forty-eight contiguous states into six groups of eight states each on the basis of per capita income levels in 1920, 1930, 1940, and 1950. He then divided the industrial structure roughly into three major sectors: agriculture, manufacturing, and services. He found that the relationship between agriculture and income is clearly negative. That is, those states with larger proportions of employment in agriculture tended almost uniformly to have significantly lower levels of income. The greater the share of the labor force in manufacturing, the higher was the level of income. Kuznets then divided manufacturing into raw materials-oriented industries (such as food and tobacco, textiles, lumber, and chemicals) and fabricating industries (such as machinery and equipment, and miscellaneous manufactures). He found that the lowest per capita income levels for states tended to be associated with relatively high proportions of raw materials industries and relatively low proportions of wages and salaries coming from the fabricating industries.

Perloff, et al. (1960) found substantially the same results in their own analyses of the relative importance of various employment categories. They calculated rank correlation coefficients for state income relative to proportions in each category. They found negative correlations between income and proportions in agriculture (−0.65) and resource-processing industries (−0.60), positive correlations with manufacturing in general (0.33) and business services (0.57), and little or no relationship between income levels and proportions in consumer services (p. 527). When they compared broadly the industrial composition of the twelve states with the highest income, they found wide variations in the economic structures. Agricultural states in the North and West tended to enjoy high incomes in spite of heavy agricultural bases; heavily agricultural southern states tended to have low incomes. They concluded that "while there is a tendency for income levels to vary from state to state with the broad classes of employment characteristic of the various states, one finds relatively high income associated with many different kinds of specialization in employment" (p. 529).

That conclusion was reinforced by a separate study by Perloff alone (Perloff 1957). In that study Perloff employed a standardization procedure across states for fifty-eight two-digit employment categories. By multiplying the proportion of known state employment by the national average income per person in each of the industry groups to obtain the level of income, adjusted for industrial structure that would be expected if national average wages were paid everywhere in the nation. Perloff found a simple correlation of 0.861 between observed per capita income and expected per capita income for the forty-eight states in 1950. But Perloff also demonstrated that there are wide variations within each broad industry category in the average wages paid. For example, the average income per employee in manufacturing as a whole (1949-51) was $4,882. The average for the apparel and other finished fabricated products (garment manufacturing) was only $2,893; and the average for products of petroleum and coal was $12,423. It is not, then, the broad category of employment that determines income levels; it is the specific industry and its relative wage level that is important. The more detailed the analysis, it appears, the more pronounced the relationship.

Perloff, et al. took the analysis one step further and investigated differences among states in labor income from specific manufacturing industries. They calculated the ratio of capital to labor for each of seventeen manufacturing industries, and then calculated the proportions of employment in each state in high-capital and low-capital industries. They found a rank correlation of 0.38 between percentage in high-capital industries and manufacturing earnings across states. Then, by means of an analysis of covariance of the relationship between wages and value added per worker, they concluded that "interstate variation in wages per production worker man-hour can be explained by differences in the marginal productivity of labor resulting from differences in the proportion with which labor is combined with other factors of production" (pp. 581-82).

This conclusion makes the urban development problem, when viewed as the selection of new industries, even more difficult. For it implies that an industry with high wages nationally may employ relatively less capital and relatively more labor in low-wage, low-skill areas. If that occurs the national wage is a poor indicator of the wages that will be paid in any given area.

Mattila and Thompson conducted an econometric analysis of income levels across 135 SMSAs for 1960. Among the variables they found to be significant in a multiple regression framework, the ratio of capital to labor, the percent of the labor force in manufacturing, and the percent of the labor force in durable-goods manufacturing were all important (Mattila and Thompson 1968, p. 65).

To What Extent Are Income Growth Rates Associated with Industrial Structure?

Rates of income change by states were also examined by Simon Kuznets. Kuznets (1958) found a positive association between the percentage growth in income per capita and the changes in the shares of the agriculture and mining sectors from 1920 to 1950. In those states that experienced the highest rise in per capita income, the decline in the share of agriculture and the rise in the share of the manufacturing sector are both greater than the average for all states. Rank correlation between increases in manufacturing as a proportion of total employment and changes in per capita income yielded a coefficient of 0.57.

George H. Borts and Jerome L. Stein (1964) also offer empirical evidence on this relationship. They note that the convergence in per capita personal income among states and major regions from 1890 to 1950 is closely associated with an increase in the proportion of the labor force in nonagricultural jobs. They show further that growth of per capita income has been greatest in those states where the wage-differentials between agricultural and nonagricultural sectors have been greatest and where the initial proportion of the low-wage sector is highest.

This is fragmentary evidence at best. One would like to know the relationship between the growth of specific industries in total output and the growth of income levels in those areas where the products are produced. But it does not appear that that study has yet been done. It is clear that those regions and cities that have enjoyed the highest increases in income have either been composed of industries with the most rapidly rising wage levels or have gained new industries with higher-than-average wage levels or have had greater-than-average shifts of the population from low-wage to high-wage industries. But it is critical to the organization of an urban development program to know which of these trends has been true most frequently and which would offer the greatest potential for development policy.

Studies of Employment and Output Growth

One of the most sophisticated analyses of metropolitan employment and the export-base hypothesis is that of Richard V. Knight (1973). The study is particularly useful for analysis of urban income levels (although Knight did not attempt such) because it focuses upon the value added per employee among industries. Value added per employee (the value of goods and services sold, less the cost of material inputs purchased from other industries, and divided by the number of employees) bears a rough relationship to wages in industries. It is not precisely related because value added must be divided between payments for capital equipment and payments to labor. But to the extent that value added per employee is high, wages will generally tend to be high.

Knight set out to analyze the magnitude and the patterns of trade among 368 cities in the United States from 1940 to 1960. Since a large proportion of all the United States population lives in these cities, he was essentially evaluating not only exports from one city to another but most exports from most major United States cities. To permit estimation of these trade flows, which are not measured or estimated by the government, Knight estimated production in each city across thirty-one industry categories by multiplying national averages for value added per employee in each category by the number employed in each city in that category. Production available for trade consists of total production less local requirements. Total local requirements were assumed equal, in each case, to the value of local wage and salary, profit, rent, and interest payments (total metropolitan factor payments), and they were allocated across industries in the same proportions as each industry contributes to national value added. These are relatively harsh assumptions, but Knight makes a plausible case for them. Estimates of exports and imports in each city were then reconverted to employment terms by means of the same value added per employee national averages. The results are, essentially, estimates of employment in each export sector of 368 cities defined on a fully comparable basis.

Knight used these estimates first to test the stability of the export-base or trade multiplier, the ratio of total metropolitan employment to employment in the export sector. That ratio is the crucial core of all export-base type analyses. Among the 368 cities studied, Knight found that the trade multiplier varied from 1.5 to 11.2. The variation seemed related to three factors: (1) the population size of the city, (2) the level of value-added per employee in the city's specific export sector, and (3) the industrial diversity of the export sector. The multiplier averaged 4.1 for cities under 200,000 and 7.6 for cities over 1.6 million. In general, the higher the value added per employee, the larger the multiplier. And the greater the diversity of production (measured by the proportion of export industry production exported), the greater the multiplier appeared to be. These three characteristics suggest that larger and more diverse cities are more self-sufficient and that higher income export sectors generate greater demand for local production.

More important, Knight found that the size of a city's multiplier "often changed significantly over the course of each decade" (p. 97). Knight concludes that economic base studies, if they are used, should make allowance for the upgrading of the export sector, loss of certain functions, and the broadening of the local production base.

Knight studied changes in employment patterns as related to trade patterns among cities. Increasing self-sufficiency of metropolitan areas was again apparent, especially in the larger areas. This is consistent with the evidence of industrial decentralization considered in the previous chapters. Analysis of job increases and job decreases in the various industries and across cities illuminated a rather clear tendency for low-productivity export industries to relocate from large and medium-sized metropolitan areas to small metropolitan areas. The larger metropolitan areas appear to have upgraded their economic bases by expanding most rapidly in four industries (printing and publishing, other transportation equipment, finance-insurance and real estate, and business and repair services) that possessed productivity levels eighteen percent above the national average.

Knight's analysis has several implications for policy, which he noted. First, the local sectors of urban economies appear to be the major source of employment expansion. Emphasis upon export sectors, especially an emphasis that assumes that the relationship of export growth to total growth is constant, is likely to overlook the principal basis for change in the urban economy. Metropolitan areas, he suggests, may perhaps be characterized best as economies in a continual state of dynamic *disequilibrium* as they adjust to changes in internal and external economic factors and as they move continually toward the hypothetical equilibrium of an unchanging world.

The need to incorporate national and regional factors in any analysis of local economic development led Knight to suggest that this task may not be feasible at the local level because of the crude state of the art, the shortage of qualified manpower, and the costs of studies of sufficient scope. But areawide planning agencies or large city planning staffs may have the resources to perform the planning functions for hinterland areas.

Perloff et al. conducted one of the largest scale analyses of regional and interstate patterns of employment change that also may shed some light on urban income levels. They utilized the so-called shift-share technique to sort out the nature of changes by major industry in employment in the forty-eight contiguous states from 1934 to 1950. The shift-share approach is a technique for standardization of growth rates in individual areas relative to growth in industries nationwide. For each area the growth that the area would have had if its component industries had grown over a specific period at the same rate as their national counterparts is calculated and compared with historical growth. This growth is called the *share, proportionality* or *industry-mix component* of growth; for if local industries had grown at the same rate as national industries, then some areas would grow more rapidly than others because of the presence of rapidly growing industries. The difference between actual local growth and the share component is called the *shift* or *differential* or *internal component* of local growth. It reflects the tendency for the region to have attracted increasing or decreasing shares through growth rates different from national averages for its component industries. The technique is merely a basis for classifying growth trends and has neither predictive nor explanatory power. It is instructive, however, because it permits quantification of the growth attributable to locational characteristics of a region, the shift components defined above, and because it demonstrates the multiplicity of industry-mix changes that can create growth in an area. An urban economy can grow in employment either by possessing rapid-growth industries and retaining a proportional share of growth, by increasing the local share of industries that grow more slowly (or even of declining industries), or by combinations of changes in rapidly growing and slowly growing industries.

Empirical analysis by Perloff et al. (1960) led them to the conclusion that growth among states was not dominated by rapidly growing industries or by states with heavy concentration in such industries. They found that the requirements of industries in terms of inputs and markets have changed, and often rapidly, so that the advantages and disadvantages of the various parts of the country (and, by extension, of the various urban areas) are subject to continuing revaluation. Florida, California, and Texas, three of the states with greatest employment growth from 1939 to 1954, displayed marked differences in the components of that growth. California gained through high positive industry-mix and regional shift growth. Florida, had almost negligible industry-mix effect but gained great increases in its share of several industries, especially services and construction linked to its phenomenal population growth. Texas grew substantially in spite of a very large *negative* industry-mix effect. Heavy dependence upon declining agriculture was replaced by an increase in mining employment (petroleum and natural gas) equal to nearly half the entire national increase over that period. Perloff et al. found generally that such changing of economic base was a more important source of growth than initial industrial composition and the initial proportions of high-growth industries. It is a fluidity of the distribution of growth implied by that factor that should be heartening to those seeking to develop an area economy over time.

To What Extent are Social Characteristics Associated with Relative Income Levels?

Otis Dudley Duncan and Albert Reiss examined the social characteristics of all urban places in the nation with 10,000 inhabitants or more as of 1950 (Duncan and Reiss 1956). They found that those places which were among the upper twenty percent in terms of level of income shared a number of distinguishing characteristics when compared low-income communities (those in the lowest twenty percent). The high-income urban places tended to have a notably larger proportion of its population of the ages twenty-one or older. Duncan and Reiss hypothesized that lower income places may have had higher levels of fertility and, therefore, a younger population. One could also suggest that the age selectivity of migration to higher income places could have accounted for the differences.

Substantially larger proportions of nonwhite persons were found in low-income places, regardless of size. Labor force participation rates tend to be higher for both males and females in high-income places. Duncan and Reiss hypothesized that states and income considerations would produce higher proportions of white-collar workers in high-income cities and towns. They found mixed results. White-collar workers tended to constitute a smaller proportion of the high-income labor force than of that found in low-income areas, with the exception of large metropolitan areas and suburban cities.

John M. Mattila and Wilbur R. Thompson concluded in the econometric analysis mentioned above, that the level of family income in large cities is most closely associated with the educational level of the inhabitants (1968, p. 77). Perloff et al. discuss additional factors related to income differentials across regions and reach conclusions similar to those of Duncan and Reiss. There do not appear to be any studies that test Thompson's hypotheses on the significance of economic power in the product market and the labor market.

To What Extent Is Income Related to Migration?

Perloff et al. have pulled together the most detailed comments on the subject; the empirical analysis undertaken by Richard F. Muth (1969) offers further evidence. Perloff and friends note, "Here we are dealing with factors and interrelationships of seemingly endless complexity, and while some parts of the picture can be brought into focus rather sharply, the larger picture introduces so many unresolved questions that we can deal with it in only a generalized and speculative manner" (p. 589). The potential effect of migration upon per capita income levels can be expected to vary with the characteristics of both those who leave an area and those who are left behind.

The historical record as summarized by Perloff et al. appears to suggest that migration within the United States has tended to dampen wage levels in rapidly growing areas and has tended to ease the problems of areas with limited opportunities. They also suggest that the forces working to reduce per capita incomes in areas higher than average appear to work more powerfully and consistently than those working for movement *upward* toward the national average.

Muth, in his orientation to labor supply and employment growth, found in his cross section of twenty-five SMSAs that employment growth and migration are significantly affected by each other. In fact, he suggests that total employment increase that comes from an increase in demand for export products is little related to the hypothetical export-base multiplier. Total employment increases depend primarily upon the extent to which an increase in employment over and above the natural increase in the labor force serves to induce in-migration.

Muth found that employment tended to increase at the same rate as in-migration and that wages in both the export and the domestic sectors, roughly defined, were established in national markets and were relatively unaffected by changes in employment. The principal determinants of increased wage levels were increases in prices linked to increases in output in excess of increases in employment. That is, wages and, consequently, per capita income were more closely related to productivity increases than to migration.

Muth's wage equation did not include a migration term and only indirect migration effects were tested. The smallness of the sample and the admitted difficulties with balky coefficients leave this as an area that also merits further analysis.

Summary

It appears that a consensus with respect to the determinants of relative urban income levels and of changes in those levels requires not the superimposition of simplified mechanical models but rather careful analysis of the characteristics of the local economy, evaluation of alternative potential sources of growth, and an awareness of the potential relationship between employment growth and migration. The following questions illustrate some of the concerns that emerge from this chapter and that may be important in the analysis of individual cities and the design of development policies:

1. To what extent are current levels of income related to special demographic characteristics of the local population?
2. To what extent are current levels of income related to special characteristics of the local labor force (relative education or skill levels), special characteristics of principal industries (market influence and unionization), or unusual employment patterns (construction booms, temporary defense spending, or unsustainable expansion of a principal industry)?
3. What industries are most likely to expand? Will they produce an increase in jobs with wages above the local average, and are these industries that are likely to encounter rising relative prices for their products in their markets?
4. To what extent will growth in employment be offset by migration into the area?
5. If local incentives (subsidies) are being extended to firms to relocate or expand, to what extent are such incentives tied to the training, retraining, or other upgrading and employment of the current local labor force rather than the employment of new in-migrants?
6. How much attention is being paid to managing or guiding the expansion of the local services sector, the principal source of new employment in most cities?
7. To what extent would industrial location subsidies be better spent in programs designed to upgrade the quality of the local labor force through vocational and professional training programs related to industries for which the area appears to have a comparative advantage?

Neither employment growth nor growth in local production nor, much less, population growth will lead to the *development* of the urban economy unless their nature, composition, and relative rates of growth correspond to the conditions suggested in this chapter. Naïve "boosterism" that proclaims that "more" means "better" in the urban economy may be justified because more may mean better *for some* (as discussed in Chapter 5), but growth that is indiscriminately encouraged may bring no benefits in terms of higher average income while it contributes to the reduction in the quality of urban life through greater congestion, higher living costs, and environmental deterioration.

4

Can Urban Income Stability be Improved?

Employment in a high-wage industry will not generate high levels of annual income if that employment is erratic. A lower wage paid in an industry with steady employment may generate higher income. For any particular wage level, the more stable the employment over the year, the higher the income level will be. Wilbur R. Thompson suggests that stability is one of three local economic goals that are appropriate bases for urban economic development efforts. He has offered the most detailed theoretical discussion available of the broad nature of instability of various kinds, of some of the possible causes, and of potential policy (1965, pp. 133-72).

Thompson distinguishes three kinds of urban instability: (1) seasonal instability, (2) cyclical instability, and (3) growth instability. In this chapter we discuss each type; we consider some of the studies that have been undertaken to explain urban instability, and we also consider some research that has been done on the possibilities for local communities to enact policies that are likely to be successful in reducing local instability. There has been very little empirical research on seasonal instability in the urban economy, virtually none on growth instability, but a sizable amount on cyclical or medium-term instability. Our survey of empirical work, therefore, emphasizes the last group of studies and centers on the concept of diversifying the urban economy.

Significance of Seasonal Instability in the Urban Economy

The so-called seasonal instability found in urban economies is of several sorts. On the one hand, it refers to fluctuations in production or employment in the area's economic base that are related to monthly or weekly differences in temperature, customs, or production processes. Increases in production in food processing industries at or after the harvest periods, Christmas peaks in retail sales, or August layoffs in the auto industry for model changes are examples of the regular predictable swings associated with seasonal instability. Seasonal fluctuations tend to receive less attention because their predictability permits both producers and employees to anticipate them and to reduce the detrimental effects. Predictable fluctu-

65

ations in the urban economy with even shorter intervals concern traffic flows, daily patterns in the use of public buildings, or weekly patterns of use for other public facilities such as lakes, beaches, or parks.

These fluctuations are of economic consequence, Thompson suggests, because they constitute relatively inefficient uses of resources. The labor force that is idled by off-season reductions in agricultural or food processing industries constitutes a resource that could be used more efficiently. Urban public infrastructure such as streets, highways, buildings, and bus systems have to be designed to handle peak loads. To the extent that there is a substantial difference between average loads and peak loads, such infrastructure will be inefficiently utilized during average load periods.

The predictability of seasonal fluctuations also simplifies the solutions required to reduce negative impacts. Seasonal demand tends to draw seasonal migrants or seasonal increases in labor force participation by persons who are able to plan to work at one occupation during some months and at another during others. To the extent that such migration and temporary changes in participation are sufficient to fill the labor needs during peak seasons, seasonal fluctuations may be of little concern. To the extent, however, that such flows and changes either do not occur with precisely the right timing and in the right magnitude, temporary distortions in local labor markets may occur. If it becomes necessary to raise wages during the working season in order to obtain the labor force needed during that period and to sustain that labor force during the off-season, the establishment of seasonally complementary industries may permit a reduction of peak-season wages and a consequent increase in local competitiveness without reducing annual incomes of local residents. The identification of such seasonally complementary industries is discussed below.

Medium-term Instability

If *seasonal instability* refers to those fluctuations in employment and output that, in addition to being predictable, are generally of short-term duration, fluctuations in the general level of economic activity over periods of several months to several years may be described as *medium-term instability*. This description of such fluctuations appears superior to the term cyclical instability for several reasons. *Cyclical instability* has been used by Thompson and others to refer to medium-term changes, but the term appears to imply that such fluctuations are necessarily associated with cycles in the national or regional economy. One of the principal activities of economists during the late 1940s and the 1950s was the search for a definition of and an explanation for business cycles. Subsequently, it has become apparent that the swings from more rapid to less rapid growth in the national economy are not components of any regular systematic cycle, but rather that each set of changes has causes that are more or less unique and that no simple explanations will reduce them to readily predictable phenomena.

Fluctuations in the national economy do appear to have substantially different effects upon different cities within the nation. Whether for that reason or for others, the differences in instability among cities is substantial. An estimate of relative instability in manufacturing employment by Michael E. Conroy (1972) indicated that for fifty-two SMSAs studied over 120 months from 1958 to 1967 the mean fluctuation around the growth trend was 4.7 percent on the labor force. The most stable city in the sample (Dallas, Texas) showed only 1.7 percent average fluctuation from month to month; the least stable city (Great Falls, Montana) experienced 19.3 percent (pp. 113-14). Various approaches to the analysis of the source of differences in fluctuations have been suggested, but explanations based on industrial composition remain intuitively most appealing.

In Thompson's words (1965, p. 16),

. . . [n]othing could seem more certain, deductively than a close causal relationship between the local industry mix and the cyclical instability of that area. Local business cycles would seem to reflect in large part the cyclical characteristics of its principal exports. . . .

The relationship between the industrial structure of a small area and the relative fluctuations it tended to encounter was noted by J. M. Clark long before regional and urban economics were in their infancy. Clark suggested that durable goods industries probably fluctuate more than nondurables because the expenditures on durables (appliances, autos, furniture, machinery) were far more sensitive to changes in income than expenditures on nondurable goods (food, clothing, entertainment, etc.). He hypothesized that overall fluctuations in local production or employment might be explained by the proportions of production or employment found in the different industrial categories (Clark 1934, p. 75). Rutledge Vining generalized on this approach in a series of articles in the 1940s (Vining 1945, 1946, and 1949). He suggested that the differences in the nature of demand for imports and exports of a region could explain the regional response to national expansion or contraction. He hypothesized that a region which exported products for which national demand was very sensitive to income changes and which tended to import products that were insensitive to income changes would suffer most. For in such a region, even if export income fell off suddenly, residents would continue importing products and the imbalance would lead to shifts in bank balances away from the area and an accelerated contraction of local economic activity.

Thompson believes that the export-base analysis that underlies Vining's suggestions leads to conclusions that are distinct from a pure industry-mix approach. The industry-mix approach suggests that each industry in an area, whether export or local, grows or declines by the same amount as its national counterpart. The local fluctuation becomes a reflection of national fluctuations that vary across cities or other regions because industry-mix varies from place to place. The export-base approach to cyclical fluctuations concentrates, reasonably enough, on the fluctuations in export industries. Contraction in exports of area products then induces contraction of local service industries whether or not such local industries are contracting nationwide. This latter approach casts the local fluctuations as "the lengthened shadow of the export industry," implying local fluctuations in excess of industry-specific fluctuations.

Does Stability Vary with City Size?

One of the more venerable discussions in the literature on urban development and urban economic structure pertains to the relationship between the diversity of the economic structure of a city, its relative stability, and its size. Otis Dudley Duncan and Albert Reiss (1956), Duncan et al. (1960), and Beverly Duncan and Stanley Lieberson (1970) have all suggested that their studies of the characteristics of cities of different size indicate that larger places tend to be more diversified in the sense that they possess a larger number of different industry types. The central place theories discussed in Chapter 2 provide a deductive basis for expecting that kind of diversity: Small places are assumed to provide a relatively narrow set of goods and services to their relatively small hinterlands. Goods and services with large hinterlands are supplied to them from other places that contain all the small-town functions plus some more specialized functions. They must also, then, be larger.

Thompson (1965, p. 147) assumes that such a relationship exists. He questions, however, whether diversity in this sense will necessarily bring greater stability. A large number of different industries is likely to reduce seasonal instability since seasonality is probably a random phenomenon. The seasonality of industries in any single location, however, is less likely to be random than that of industries nationally, especially where the seasonality is related to the agricultural resource base or other locational characteristics specific to that place.

But cyclical or medium-term instability is a distinct phenomenon. Increases and decreases in production or employment in a set of industries over the medium term (say, one to three years) are not likely to be independent or randomly distributed. They tend, rather, to be linked with common national increases and decreases. Industrial diversification would then seem, according to Thompson, to be a process of averaging the responses of industries to national cycles. Industrial diversification would lead toward a cycle approximating that of the nation as a whole. To the extent that large urban economies contain a more representative sample of the nation's industries they should tend to have stability more or less identical to that of the nation. Smaller urban economies should exhibit a much greater range of instability over the medium term, for some tend to specialize in the more unstable and some in the more stable industries.

One problem that the analysis of diversification with respect to city size tends to accentuate is the nature of the diversity that should be associated with greater relative stability. If one tends merely to count the number of different industries, the question arises: In what sense should industries be different? If one wishes to measure the contribution of an industry to regional fluctuations, is it sufficient to assume that the Standard Industrial Classification (S.I.C.) system separates industry into groups that are sufficiently and appropriately different for purposes of measuring their relative contributions to aggregate fluctuations? Probably not. In the first place, the S.I.C. system was never intended for such purposes. Industries are classified on the basis of very general characteristics in terms of inputs, products, and processes. Diversification requires that industries be differentiated on the basis of their respective tendencies to increase or decrease regional stability.

One approach to the instability and diversification problem that confronts this problem is that of Michael E. Conroy (1972). Conroy proposed that individual industries need to be weighted by an index of their relative national tendencies to fluctuate. Empirical analysis with this weighted measure, discussed below, tended to suggest much greater explanatory power for the industry-mix approach than was previously noted.

Growth Instability

In the previous chapter we considered the determinants of levels and growth rates of urban incomes. Thompson suggests that fluctuations in rates of growth over long periods (say, five to twenty years) may be viewed as a form of instability of considerable concern to an urban area. Growth instability refers to fluctuations in the growth trend for the urban economy as a whole. The planning of public and private investment in the area requires some knowledge of the likely trends, and the greater the instability in those trends, the more likely it is that those investments will be made inefficiently, either exceeding or falling short of needs. The policy prescription is simple: One needs to generate a local industry mix of complementary growth trends, a mix of young, mature, and decadent industries. If that mix is associated with the larger cities, one should expect large cities to have the most stable growth trends over the long run.

The actual problem is somewhat more severe. For one needs to identify not merely a mix of national industries that will tend to grow, mature, and decline at complementary differing rates; one must identify industries that will grow, mature, and decline at different rates *in a specific location,* the city with which one is concerned. We noted in the previous chapter the rather severe problems associated with identifying specific, narrowly defined industries that will tend to produce high income levels in any specific city. National growth rates are no more likely to predict local growth than are national wage levels likely to foretell local wages in the industry. There is some correspondence, but it is highly unreliable.

Empirical Studies of Urban and Other Regional Instability and Local Economic Characteristics

Phillip Neff and Annette Weifenbach explored similarities and differences in the timing, duration, and amplitude of cycles in six major industrial urban areas over the period from 1914 to 1945 (Neff and Weifenbach 1949). They constructed bar-graphs for each city that permitted comparison of the peaks and troughs of local cycles with similar points in national trends. They then compared the graphs visually and attempted to relate the relative local cycles to a few gross characteristics of the industrial structure of each city. They determined that the industrial pattern appeared related to local fluctuations, but "not in any simple and direct manner." There was no relationship apparent between rate of growth and fluctuations, and industrial specialization appeared significant only in extreme cases. But one could also suggest that the empirical technique was so rough that the relationship could be observed only in extreme cases.

A later empirical study by Robert M. Williams improved on that technique. Williams calculated rank correlation coefficients for the relationship between the percent of manufacturing wage earners in non-durable manufacturing industries (presumably the more stable industries) and an index of stability based on retail sales for a bad year during the Depression (1933) compared with the average over the Depression years (1939-37) for thirteen cities. He found significant relationship between the two, but both measures that he used were questionable (cf. Conroy 1972, pp. 15-17).

Frank A. Hanna attempted to "separate and measure [the] combination of cyclical, secular, and random elements in state per capita income (Hanna 1954). He used an index of sensitivity (the percentage change in state income divided by percentage change in national income over a number of years) to analyze the relationship between industrial structure and relative fluctuations. He found that states with high proportions of employment in agriculture tended to be more sensitive to changes in national income than those states with high proportions in durable and nondurable goods manufacture. Rutledge Vining (1945) predicted this by noting that a large proportion of agriculture today consists either of products that are primarily industrial inputs (e.g., cotton or soybeans) or of food products that are sensitive to income changes (e.g., meat products).

George H. Borts conducted the most comprehensive study to date of state employment fluctuation (Borts 1961). Borts analyzed relative state fluctuations for three periods of business contraction and expansion as related to state industrial structure. He standardized the state patterns by calculating for each state the cycle the nation would have had over those periods if it had had the state's industrial composition. He concluded that the states whose industrial composition would have given the nation the greatest fluctuations (the most variable states) were those characterized by a high proportion of durable goods manufacture, specifically transportation equipment, primary and fabricated metal products, machinery and lumber. Nondurable manufactures characterized the least-variable states. Borts' study has been criticized because he was led to assume that each state industry would behave in the same fashion as its national counterpart. But that could occur only if there were no intermediate production (products used as inputs by other factories) in any state or if the patterns of intermediate production were identical in every state. This was an excessively-narrow industry-mix formulation that precluded the possibility of differently multiplied effects in states with different industrial composition. Although Borts did not quantify the explanatory power of the industrial structure variable, he qualified his findings very heavily. Given that his technique was likely to have underestimated the full effects, further analysis was called for.

Richard A. Siegel incorporated a stronger measure of regional stability into an analysis of fluctuations in thirty-one SMSAs over the 1949-62 period (Siegel 1966) and found a rank correlation coefficient of 0.71 between a measure of average fluctuations and the percentage of total manufacturing employment in durable goods industries.

Addison T. Cutler and James E. Hansz constructed a sensitivity index for thirty-five metropolitan areas based on acceleration and deceleration of growth in bank debits and nonagricultural employment (measures of overall urban production) from 1961 to 1968. They then calculated simple correlation coefficients between this index and three measures of industrial structure: durable goods as percent of manufacturing, 0.361; durable goods as a percent of total employment, 0.449; and manufacturing as a share of total employment, 0.337 (Cutler and Hansz 1971).

Urban Industrial Diversification

What type of industrial structure is characteristic of the more stable urban economies? If, in general, specialization in durable goods industries will tend to produce a less stable economic structure, can one simply avoid durable industries and reduce fluctuations? Durable goods as a category of industries includes a very large range of different industries, some of which may be more stable than some nondurable industries. Again, we confront the need to look at more detailed industries.

Several alternative measures of industrial diversity or diversification for urban areas have been proposed to cope with the dual problems: How should one separate industries usefully, and how much of each industry should be associated with greater stability? The first two present common conceptual problems; they do not specify precisely either the form of instability against which one is diversifying, and they presuppose that there should exist a norm for the measurement of diversification. The third overcomes these problems to some extent.

P. Sargent Florence (1948), W. Steigenga (1955), and (implicitly) George H. Borts (1961) calculated specialization and diversification relative to the proportions of industry in the national economy. To the extent that an area contained significantly greater proportions of an industry than the national economy it was assumed to be *specialized* in that industry. Perfect diversification consisted of just duplicating the national average. But if an area was heavily oriented to very stable industries, would it not be diversified in a meaningful sense, even though this measure would not show it?

Glenn E. McLaughlin (1930), R. C. Tress (1938), and A. Rodgers (1957) studied diversification by measuring deviation of the proportions of various industries in an area from an equal distribution across all industries. Their approach, also referred to as the "ogive" or cumulative distribution approach, suffered from the specific defect that the diversified proportion of any industry varied, depending on the number of industries studied.

The use of S.I.C. categories introduces the problem, discussed above, of the nature of the differences among industries that those categories reflect.

More serious, however, is the problem of assuming that for any economically meaningful purpose there will be a normal amount of industry in any local area. If that concept has relevance, it does so only where the geographical size of the market is very small. One would expect every city of a specific size to have a normal quantity of an industry only if the market area was no larger than that city. For if any industry could serve not only the population of its immediate hinterland but also some of the population of contiguous or further regions, then it would be unreasonable to expect that all regions would have identical quantities or any fixed quantity of an industry. To measure industrial diversification relative to a norm in terms of expected or balanced distributions might be appropriate for those industries that are essentially locally oriented. But the industries that are capable of serving as a vehicle for transmission of fluctuations from the national economy to the local urban economy are the export industries that necessarily have market areas larger than that of the city in which they are producing.

Michael E. Conroy (1972) has suggested an approach to the definition and analysis of urban industrial diversity that appears to overcome some of these difficulties. Conroy begins from the premise that the objective of diversification is to reduce the fluctuations in economic activity in specific urban economies. The contribution of each industry in the industry-mix to total fluctuations in the area, he hypothesized, consists of the magnitude of its contribution to employment or regional income weighted by its relative tendency to fluctuate. That tendency to fluctuate, he suggested, has two distinguishable components: (1) the industry's own tendency to fluctuate nationally, *plus* (2) its linkages to other industries in the area.

If one ignores these linkages, as Borts did, one overlooks a potentially very important source of differences in urban stability. For an industry within a specific city could fluctuate more than the national average simply because the set of industries that it is supplying locally is different from the national industrial structure. For example, a fall in the national demand for commercial aircraft might reduce demand by an equal percent in each of three aircraft-oriented cities. But it would have a greater impact upon overall regional fluctuations in one region if a large proportion of the firms that supply the final airframe industry are also located there.

Conroy drew concepts and techniques from the literature on diversification of stock portfolios to suggest that industrial diversification is an analogous problem. Just as stockbrokers attempt to pool the risk associated with individual issues, Conroy suggested that urban planners should view industrial diversification as the pooling of the risk of fluctuations in output and employment. He proposed that the weights to be used in summing the contribution of individual industries to total urban fluctuations should be measures of historical instability (such as the variance); and that a potentially appropriate indirect measure of the effect of industrial linkages upon fluctuations would be the covariances between industries as measured at the national level. When the proportions of, say, employment in each industry in an area are multiplied by the variances and covariances, these can be summed to yield a single aggregate measure of expected fluctuations for each city, the "industrial portfolio variance." This is a standardization procedure that is not greatly different from that used by Victor R. Fuchs (1967) to study relative earnings levels, by Harvey S. Perloff (1957) to study the relationship between industrial composition and state income levels, or by George H. Borts (1961) to study relative state sensitivity to national cycles. Here each city is given the average amount of fluctuation that it could expect if its industries fluctuated the same as they do nationally and if local interindustry fluctuations were the same as their national counterparts.

Conroy also offered the industrial portfolio variance as an alternative index of industrial diversification. This index tends to correspond more closely with the economic objective of diversification than it does to the common sense notion of diversity. A diversified economy in Conroy's sense is one that has an industrial structure which has low aggregate expected fluctuations. It could conceivably consist of only two or three stable industries with very low fluctuations themselves (low variances) and virtually no interrelation with one another (zero covariances). Or a diversified economy could consist of one that included several large unstable industries (high variances) that tended to expand and contract in response to opposite national trends (high negative covariances). In that case expansion of one industry would be expected at the time that the other was contracting with the net result of overall stability so long as the labor force was capable of moving relatively easily from one to the other.

As an index or measure of diversification, the industrial portfolio variance could be formulated to reflect diversification of various sorts. If one wishes to diversify with respect to seasonal instability, one need only calculate the national variances and covariances across data on seasonal fluctuations by industry to build an index specific to that purpose. If one wished to work on growth instability to diversify an economy for the long haul, however, one would need long-term data and a modicum of fortitude. For the assumption implicit in the use of national industry data to predict local area fluctuations may be tenable when dealing with the short-term seasonal or medium-term fluctuations that appear to be more closely associated with industry characteristics than local characteristics; but it is perhaps heroic when looking at five-, ten-, and twenty-year projections of local growth.

This measure also provides insight into the relationship between diversified cities and national fluctuations. Thompson had suggested that the diversified city tended toward relative fluctuations identical to those of the nation. But that conclusion was predetermined by his implicit definition of diversification by comparison with national industrial proportions. With the industrial portfolio approach, it is possible to see how a city might be more diversified than the nation, how the reduction of instability in a number of cities simultaneously would not necessarily mean competition for the few stable industries, and how, in fact, careful diversification programs nationwide could tend to reduce national fluctuations. A city could be more diversified than the nation by means of one of many alternative economic structures that produce aggregate expected fluctuations which are less than those of the nation. This would not necessarily consist of vicious interregional competition for a few stable industries. The industry that, through local acquisition or expansion, would reduce expected fluctuations most in any specific city would depend on both the preexisting industrial structure of the city and the characteristics of the industry itself (in terms of variance and covariances with the preexisting industries). Two cities would be likely to compete for precisely the same industry, in terms of diversification, only if they had essentially identical preexisting industrial structures and similar locational characteristics. Finally, fluctuations in the national economy have no independent life of their own. They consist of the weighted average of individual state and local fluctuations. To the extent that urban development programs oriented to diversification tend to reduce local area fluctuations, the national average will also be reduced.

Are Diversified Cities More Stable?

Apparently the only empirical analysis available to date that tests alternative indices of industrial diversification against indices of historical instability is that of Conroy (1972). In that study Conroy gathered monthly manufacturing employment data for the 120-month period from January 1958 to December 1967 with respect to fifty-two United States SMSAs. From that he calculated indices of historical fluctuation around the ten-year growth trend as measures of relative cyclical or medium-term instability. For each city he then estimated 1963 employment in each of 118 manufacturing industry groups, and he calculated measures of diversification for each city based on the national average approach (comparison with national average share of employment in each industry), the balanced or ogive approach (comparison with identical proportions in all industries), and on the basis of the percent of employment in durable goods industries.

To these he added estimates of his industrial portfolio variance measure of relative diversification. They were calculated using national employment data in the same 118 industries for the same 120-month period to determine expected instability of individual industries and industry mixes. Cross-section comparison of relative historical fluctuations and the respective indices of diversification by means of simple correlation and regression analysis indicated that diversification according to the national average, ogive, and percent-durable measures was very little related to historical instability. The correlation coefficients were 0.163, 0.261, and 0.083, respectively, for the principal data series. The portfolio variance measure, however, exhibited a coefficient of 0.658. Regression analysis only confirmed that conclusion. The portfolio variance measure explained forty-two percent of the cross-section variation in instability; the national average measure accounted for only seven percent, the ogive measure five percent and the percent durable virtually none.

The conclusion relevant to stabilization planning appeared clear:

> Whether the explanatory power of industrial diversification as measured by the portfolio variance . . . is sufficient to justify (or re-establish the validity of) using industrial structure as a diversification instrument for stabilization policy will depend upon the preferences and alternatives of the policy-maker. It would appear doubtful that any other *single* factor can be expected to account for as much as 42% of the variation in a cross section as small as 52 cities. In the opinion of the author, such significance . . . lends more-than-adequate credibility to a policy of careful diversification in order to stabilize regional economies [Conroy 1972, pp. 143–44].

Are Large Cities Either More Diversified or More Stable?

Frank Clemente and Richard B. Sturgis (1971) tested the relationship between diversification and size for 535 United States communities in 1960. They used an index based on the balanced structure approach, assuming that perfect diversification consisted of equal proportions in each of twelve industries. They found a correlation of 0.41 between their index and city size for the whole sample, and from 0.36 in the Southeast to 0.55 in the West.

Ronald W. Crowley (1973) reflected on the Clemente and Sturgis results, noting that their measure of diversification is only one of several and that their sample of cities may have been biased toward small cities. Using additional data for all Canadian cities with population above 25,000 and an unspecified number of industries, he then estimated correlation coefficients between population size and labor force size and six different measures of specialization without much discussion of each. The measures were (1) the proportion of employment in the three largest industries, (2) the reciprocal of the number of industries required to account for eighty percent of the labor force, (3) the ogive measure discussed above, (4) a modified measure of squared excesses over national average, (5) a measure of relative industry shares based on the national average approach, and (6) a complex measure of differences among cities in their deviations from the national average base.

Crowley found that "only measures of *internal* specialization appear to be significantly correlated with size." Those measures that relate to the external characteristics, such as national average or comparative structures show little or no relationship. The correlation coefficients calculated by Crowley ranged from −0.01 to −0.52 for 1961 (the negative signs are correct since smaller values of the indices mean greater diversification). The labor force as a measure of size yields higher correlation coefficients than sheer population, but the explanatory power of all the indices fell sharply from 1951 to 1961. This suggests, again, that city structures were becoming more heterogeneous and, perhaps, that the decentralization seen in the United States was also being experienced by Canadian cities.

In the analysis of diversification and instability undertaken by Conroy (1972) and discussed above, there was also some evidence on the relationship between the size of population and of the manufacturing labor force and diversification within the manufacturing sector. Conroy found uniformly low correlations between both measures of size and the four indices of diversification discussed above. The national average measures similar to those used by Crowley and by Clemente and Sturgis yielded the highest correlations (−0.305 and −0.294, for population and labor force, respectively). The portfolio variance approach exhibited lower coefficients (−0.170 and −0.178, for the principal data series). But none of these relationships were statistically significant at the conventional ten percent level. That is, there was a greater than ten percent probability that random factors in a sample of that size (fifty-two) could have generated the coefficients encountered.

A more important critique of the relationship was found when Conroy tested the relationship between relative historical instability, industrial diversification, and city size. Using multivariate regression analysis, Conroy discovered that neither the size of a city's population nor the size of its manufacturing labor force makes a significant additional contribution (after relative diversification) to the explanation of variation across cities in historical manufacturing employment fluctuations. City size, then, was significantly related to neither diversification nor to historical instability in the manufacturing sectors.

Conroy's sample may have been biased toward the larger cities, for the population of the metropolitan areas within it ranged from 73,000 to 10.6

million; the average size was 1.2 million; and there were only six urban areas under 200,000. The reduced significance of city size may also have been related to the use of manufacturing sector data alone. The relationships among historical fluctuations, city size, and more general diversification remain to be tested.

The policy relevance of city size to urban development programs remains to be evaluated. Even if size and stability were closely related, there is no data yet available on the extent to which the growth of a city from any given size to another may be expected to stabilize the economic base. If, as Conroy's data show, some small- or medium-sized cities have had relatively stable industry mixes and if population growth brings undesirable side effects, to what extent is growth for the sake of diversification and stability a costly way to achieve it? That will depend, to some extent, on the extent to which diversification is feasible by direct action upon the industrial structure.

To What Extent Can Urban Stability be Improved by Diversification Policy?

Virtually every Chamber of Commerce brochure that describes local industrial development efforts alludes to local interest in diversifying the local economy. Presumably a significant portion of all industrial development funds are allocated to efforts in that direction. But there appear to be no studies that have been undertaken to evaluate actual attempts to diversify local structures or of their relative success in reducing instability. One recent theoretical and empirical analysis, however, has shed some light on the potential impact of diversification policy.

In two separate papers Conroy has suggested that the diversification potential of a new or expanded industry creates benefits for the local economy that the new or expanded plants are unable to reap, that for that reason some form of industrial location subsidy may be justified to attract diversifying industries, and that such subsidies, if effective in drawing the industries needed, could reduce fluctuations significantly (Conroy 1974a, 1974b).

The need for a diversification location subsidy is based upon the suggestion that reduction of fluctuations in the local economy will lead to a reduction in the real wage necessary to retain the labor force in that area. If fluctuations in employment, at a given wage level, generate less income over the year for the workers employed in one city than they would receive in a second city that possesses a more stable industry mix, then higher wages will be required in the first to generate an equivalent level of welfare and to keep the labor force from migrating. Any reduction in local instability would permit a reduction in wages (without reducing welfare) and an increase in local locational advantages. To the extent that firms are linked with one another and that laborers consider not only the employment patterns of a single industry, the expansion of an existing plant or firm or the acquisition of a new plant that stabilizes aggregate urban income and employment will permit not only that one plant to lower wages but, Conroy suggests, all plants in the area to some extent. The newly locating or expanding establishment reaps the benefits of the wage reduction only in terms of its own labor force. It cannot internalize or charge other establishments for the benefits they derive. For this reason Conroy suggests that subsidies to diversifying industries (or taxes on destabilizing industries) may be needed (1974b).

The ability of such subsidies to effect some diversification and for that to reduce materially the instability of an area were addressed by Conroy in a separate study (1974a). The study addresses two dimensions of the problem. First, as we noted above, Thompson doubted the effectiveness of diversification efforts since all cities would presumably be attempting to attract the same few stable industries. Conroy tested whether the potentially most diversifying industries were either the industries that were most stable nationally or were the same for three different cities. Second, in response to the potential efficacy of the policy, Conroy simulated the allocation of growth in the labor force to the optimally diversifying industries and estimated the likely reduction in average unemployment levels for three cities.

The analysis of potential diversification effect was built upon Conroy's industrial portfolio variance approach, which estimated the theoretical instability of an area on the basis of its industrial composition and the national stability of its component industries. For three cities with high historical and theoretical indices of instability and substantially different economic structures (Detroit, Michigan—manufacturing; Great Falls, Montana—mining; and Stockton, California—food processing), Conroy simulated the impact upon theoretical instability of increases of five percent, ten percent, and fifteen percent of the total labor force allocated to each of 118 manufacturing industries. He then compared the simulated effects with a ranking of national industries arranged from most stable to least stable. He found the national stability or instability had little or no relationship to the simulated stabilizing or destabilizing effect. The principal reason was that the effect of expanding any single industry depends upon the whole prior industrial structure and the relationship of the variability of the expanded industry to all of the preexisting employment sources.

Conroy found, for example, that increments of employment in grain mill products—the most variable of all manufacturing industries nationally

—would produce a greater *reduction* in instability than any of the five nationally least-variable industries. Some industries that would reduce instability at one level of expansion, say five percent, would tend to *increase* instability at a higher level such as fifteen percent.

The indexes of expected instability calculated by Conroy were related by him directly to probable levels of unemployment in each city. So long as the labor force is assumed to grow along the long-run trend of the number of jobs available, negative deviation from that trend (jobs fewer than workers) will be tantamount to unemployment. For each city one is then able to convert the index of instability to a measure of the unemployment expected with various levels of probability. By means of a mathematical programming approach, Conroy estimated the potential reduction in expected unemployment levels associated with the optimal allocation of five percent, ten percent, and fifteen percent labor force growth over all possible industries within the 118 industry classification. He found that for five percent increases in available labor such diversification effort would theoretically reduce unemployment levels, in Detroit by 17.4 percent, in Great Falls by 28.5 percent, and in Stockton by 20.2 percent. Allocation of larger increases were capable of substantially greater theoretical reductions.

Such potential effects may be misleading, however, for Conroy assumed that all industries were free to locate anywhere. Though it may be possible that large and prolonged subsidy could permit the location of citrus orchards in Greenland, the magnitude of the necessary subsidy is likely to outweigh any potential benefits. The approach appears useful, however, for it permits identification and ranking of potentially diversifying industries from among which planners might choose locationally appropriate ones.

Summary

The diversification of the economic structure of an urban economy thus appears to be a considerably more complex process than simply finding new industries that are in some vague way different from preexisting industries in an urban area. At the same time it appears that models are evolving that can be very specifically useful to planners for evaluating the relationship between current instability in employment and income and the potential stabilizing or destabilizing effect of a new or expanded plant or firm. Diversification, when viewed in this new framework, does not necessarily mean many different industries. Rather, it relates, once again, to the relationship between detailed characteristics of the existing economic structure and the specific characteristics of proposed new growth.

5 Issues in Urban Development and Income Distribution

The third arbitrarily chosen criterion identified at the beginning of this book as a basis for evaluating the quality of life associated with alternative economic structures in urban areas was the interpersonal distribution of income. The importance of income distribution as a welfare consideration is based upon an assumption that individuals do not generally determine whether or not they are satisfied with their economic conditions on the basis of the absolute level of their earnings from all sources and in isolation from the earnings received by others. Rather, most of us base some significant proportion of the satisfaction derived from our income levels (and the levels of material and nonmaterial consumption they permit) on comparisons of our levels of income with those of others around us, with those who have preceded us (parents, earlier generations), and with whatever we know of the levels of others far from us. If such is true, it could follow that greater equality in the distribution is directly related to more favorable impressions of the quality of life. Such a conclusion may not be true under conditions where, for example, preferences with respect to quality of life are weighted by income as, for instance, when public policy making is dominated by wealthy citizens. Assuming, nonetheless, that greater equality in the distribution of income is a policy objective that is accepted as readily as higher levels of income or greater stability in income flows, there are many questions and few answers that arise with respect to urban economic development.

The fact that different members of the urban community have different levels of income, different sources of income, different tastes, and different goals, and that urban economic development efforts may not benefit all equally raises another group of questions about the distribution of benefits from any given development plan or policy. In this chapter we look first at the meager amount of theoretical and empirical information available on the relationship between economic structure and the distribution of income in urban places. We then consider some of the distributional issues involved in formulating, implementing, and evaluating alternative urban economic development programs. The consideration is largely speculative, for although we identified that area as a critical one for literature review and evaluation, our literature search has turned up virtually no treatment of the questions raised.

Urban Structure and Income Inequality

Wilbur R. Thompson, once again, has pioneered in both theorizing and analyzing empirically the nature, the magnitude, and the determinants of urban income inequality. The study of income distribution, he wrote in 1965, is, in general, "perhaps the most underdeveloped area in the world of economics." His discussion of the subject constituted one of the shortest chapters in his book. In approaching the topic with respect to urban economics he found "very little literature to summarize and evaluate, with almost no empirical findings to report. . . ." (p. 105). The situation has changed little since then. Our literature search has identified only three empirical studies since then, including one by Thompson, with scant improvement over the hypotheses first raised by him.

Thompson hypothesized that greater inequality would be associated with (a) larger city size, (b) certain industry mixes, (c) socioeconomic characteristics frequently picked up in a region variable, (d) slow economic growth, and (e) high relative instability (1965, pp. 105-33). Larger cities should be expected to have greater inequality for three reasons: First, he suggested, the greater range of quality in the human resources found among big city residents should provide a basis for wider disparity. If, as migration studies show, small cities tend to lose their brightest, most aggressive, and most talented young people to the larger cities, then this loss to the small town would reduce its proportion of persons with high income potential and the simultaneous gain of the large city should increase the proportion capable of earning high incomes. The employment opportunities for poorly educated and unskilled laborers is likely to be broader in large cities than in small ones. Once again, the weights given to extreme ends of the distribution decrease for the small city and increase for the large. Second, the large city is more likely to be able to generate demand for both highly trained and poorly trained labor force. If agglomeration economies generate higher productivity, the wages available are likely to be higher for both groups in large cities than in small, thereby maintaining the flow that widens the distribution in one and narrows it in the other. Large cities are more likely to offer those with high property incomes, the very rich, a diversified set of products and services on which to spend such income. This again would tend toward greater inequality. The one counterhypothesis Thompson felt compelled to raise pertains to the availability of second jobs or jobs for second wage earners in a family. If opportunities for moonlighting and opportunities for spouses to participate in the labor force are greater in large cities than in small and if the propensity to moonlight and the propensity for both spouses to work is greater among low-income families, then that dimension would lead one to expect some mitigation of the other factors.

Industry mix could be related to income inequality in several ways, according to Thompson. If a community is dominated by a single industry that has little differentiation in wage levels, income inequality would probably be less. Cities specialized in high-wage manufacturing industries should similarly have relatively homogeneous family income levels due to the interdependence of wage levels among industries. Cities with diversified economic bases (in his terms, a large number of different industries) would, we are led to believe, expect a wider range of earnings levels and greater inequality. The amount of unionization in the industry mix is also a homogenizing factor for incomes, according to Thompson, in part because unionization is closely associated with branch plant, assembly operations and because such firms, he believes, require a relatively narrow range of skills (1968, p. 48).

Rapid economic growth in an economy should tend to reduce inequality, according to Thompson, because it creates incentives for employers who are faced with labor shortages to upgrade the quality of the labor force through training programs. It appears to be implicit in this hypothesis, however, that the rapid economic growth is *not* matched by comparable population growth. To the extent that the increased demand for labor is met by means of either the upgrading discussed by Thompson or by means of increases in local participation rates of those in lower income brackets, economic growth may reduce inequality for it raises local wage or family income levels. It would also appear to be a corollary of that analysis that an urban economy with labor force growth in excess of new job creation will encounter worsening income inequality.

Thompson has also suggested that greater stability should breed greater equality. The reasoning here runs from higher annual incomes derived from a given wage level if it is paid over more stable employment patterns. But, as we discussed in the preceding chapter, if greater relative instability implies that higher wages must be paid to retain the labor force, the effect of instability upon equality becomes ambiguous. Furthermore, if larger cities are more diversified and diversified cities are more stable, the concurrence of large size and diversification (both implying inequality) and stability (implying greater equality) creates a conundrum.

A human-capital theory approach to the problem has been proposed by H. E. Frech III and L. S. Burns (1971). By their reasoning an individual's income level depends upon innate ability and human capital investment (education, training) in himself or herself. The more developed the markets for capital, the more likely it is that individuals will invest in themselves to similar degrees. Large cities with high incomes could be expected to have the most developed markets for human capital; hence, they expect *less* inequality in large and/or high income cities.

The empirical evidence to clarify this confusing set of hypotheses is skimpy at best. Thompson calculated indices of income inequality for 151 SMSAs, using a measure of "interquartile variation," that is, the difference between income levels at the twenty-fifth and seventy-fifth percentiles, expressed as a proportion of the sum of the two. He found that the ten urban areas with the least inequality (as of 1950) were all northern manufacturing cities. The ten urban areas with the most inequality were all in the South. Correlation coefficients between proportion in manufacturing and the degree of income equality were high and positive, whether or not southern cities were included (1965, pp. 110-11).

In a separate empirical study of 135 SMSAs, John M. Mattila and Wilbur R. Thompson found that family income inequality, also measured by interquartile variations, was directly related to the proportion of the population that was nonwhite and to inequality in average educational levels. Similarly, the higher the proportion of the labor force in manufacturing and the greater the proportion of the labor force that was female, the less was the inequality. Median income levels were negatively related to inequality, that is, higher incomes were found in cities with less inequality. Population size did not enter the stepwise regression equation for income inequality; the implication is that it had no significant relationship.

Barbara B. Murray conducted a separate study of inequality across cities in levels of income (Murray 1969). She used the same measure of income differences as Thompson for an arbitrary set of fifteen large SMSAs. Without attempting correlation analysis, she inferred from the general characteristics of various subgroups that one could reach three conclusions, all of which support Thompson's findings above. First, the relatively high income cities tended to have less income inequality; second, those areas with the greatest proportions of nonwhite families tended to have greater inequality; the four metropolitan areas with less inequality all tended to have greater equality in the distribution of income.

H. E. Frech III and L. S. Burns improved upon Murray's analysis by placing her variables and her sample of cities in a multiple regression framework within which the relative significance of the various variables could be determined. They used a Gini coefficient as the measure of inequality, a superior measure; and they amplified Murray's sample to include 192 additional SMSAs. They tested the explanatory power of the same three key variables: (1) mean family income, (2) percent employed in manufacturing, and (3) percent nonwhite. The income variable was consistently the most important determinant of relative inequality. The other two variables were closely related, but their relative significance was slight (Frech and Burns 1971, p. 106). They did not test their human-capital approach more thoroughly.

Joseph P. Newhouse has provided an important more sophisticated test of the relationship between industry mix and income distribution that led him to the conclusion that "factors other than industry mix are either not important in determining the shape of the income distribution or are correlated with industry mix. . . ." (Newhouse 1971, p. 73). Newhouse tested whether the proportion of incomes in any specific income size class in an area is equal to the sum over industries of the relative number of jobs in the area that nationally generate annual incomes in that range. In one sense he is testing two things simultaneously: that the national average income for a specific job in a specific industry is paid in all areas, and that the structure of jobs does not change across the nation within industries. In other words, he is asking whether retail trade employs approximately the same proportion of clerks and pays all clerks approximately the same wages across the nation. One would expect that such an hypothesis would have relatively weak explanatory power on the basis of our discussions above of the regional variations in wage levels, regional variations in the age of plants, the technology embodied in them, and, consequently, expected differences in the occupational composition and the wage distribution of jobs in each industry. If his analysis stands the test of more finely grained testing, he has shown us how income distribution measures can be used directly in urban economic development planning.

Some of the industry-specific hypotheses discussed above were also supported. Newhouse demonstrated that the job and income composition of heavy industry (specifically: machinery, fabricated metal products, electrical equipment and instruments) are negatively associated with the proportions of population with incomes below $6,000. For middle income ranges ($9,000 to 25,000), employment in retail trade and agriculture is negatively associated, that is, the greater the proportion of employment in such heavy industry, the smaller will be the expected proportions of income earners with incomes below $6,000 per year. High proportions of employment in retail trade or agriculture imply smaller shares of middle income persons.

More important, the analysis shows that development planners may estimate the impact upon the existing distribution of any proposed economic growth, whether expansion or new location, by estimating the income range of both the direct and the indirect employment to be created. This ability, as we shall note below, may be essential to the design and analysis of development programs that are responsive to specific local needs.

The treatment of problems of income distribution remains the least developed of the topics in urban economic development policy formulation. Thompson's evidence on educational inequality offers one route for approaching the problem. But there is no evidence whether public programs to reduce income inequality by means of education are likely to be more or less efficient than direct programs of industrial development. The relationship between increased income levels and increased inequality may be interpreted to mean that income equality could become a concern that is left to resolve itself as income levels are increased overall. But the statistical evidence is such that it is possible that increased income levels on average could be associated with worsening relative levels for some segments of the urban population. Urban development planners would presumably want to avoid that possibility, but the state of our knowledge does not even permit the design of an income-increasing program that would avoid that with certainty.

For Whom Will Urban Development Programs be Undertaken?

To base an urban development program on the simple objectives of increasing average levels of income in an urban area or of stabilizing average levels overlooks the fact that those goals can be achieved by designing development programs to benefit a multiplicity of different groups within the urban economy. Just as a program to decrease hard-core unemployed will raise per capita income by benefiting low-income groups, a program to increase employment of technical and managerial persons will, in the absence of in-migration, lead to increases in the incomes of middle and upper-middle income groups. For whom should development programs be undertaken, and who will actually benefit? The answer to the first question must be written in each community by the citizens of that community. The answer to the second question is more amenable to analysis here.

Incomes come in various forms: Wage and salary incomes, profits, interest, rent, and payments are the most frequent varieties. Conflicts with respect to the goals of urban economic development may depend in large part on the source of one's income. Population growth, for example, may tend to be favored by those whose incomes come primarily from profits and rent. The owners of retail businesses earn higher profits when population growth increases demand for their products or services while simultaneously depressing local wage levels. Owners of real estate may benefit from increases in property value and increases in rents so long as population growth continues more rapidly than the clearing of new land or the construction of new structures. Wage earners have reason to resist population growth because it is likely to depress wage increases below that which would occur, especially in local services in tighter labor markets. Even among wage earners there may be conflict over growth in population. Some employed in population-sensitive industries such as retail sales, real estate, and construction may view rapid population growth as the key to their personal career progress, while those employed in nationally or regionally oriented industries for which local population growth has little impact on demand may find their wages growing more slowly because of the influx. Is it surprising that Chambers of Commerce and other "booster" organizations tend to be more heavily manned by owners and high-level employees of local retail, real estate, and construction firms?

The lack of studies of these distributional dimensions of urban economic structures is remarkable. The only study that is even tangentially related and that we have been able to find is a purely theoretical model by Peter S. Albin of unbalanced urban growth and potential intensification of the urban crisis (Albin 1971). Albin developed a theoretical approach in which problems of changing technology, poverty, and "ghettoization," education, location, and strained urban budgets are interrelated as consequences of a particular pattern of general industrial development and economic growth. It serves as an excellent intuitive example of how industrialization and growth, for all that they may generate higher incomes for *some,* may not be in the interest of the majority in an urban economy.

Albin's model, which is presented in very succinct algebraic form, may be explained intuitively as follows. Imagine a city with two export industries, one of which is technologically progressive (in terms of fairly rapid increases in productivity) and the other relatively stagnant. In the industry with increasing productivity, money wages may increase continually without putting pressure on the final cost of the product; but parallel increases in the stagnant industry would, most likely, force increases in price and reductions in production and employment. Assume that the progressive industry uses labor with considerably higher educational attainment, so that workers cannot simply cross from the stagnant industry to the progressive one as a gap develops between wage levels in the two. Over the long run, presumably some of the labor force in the stagnant industry would be able to meet the entry requirements of the progressive industry; but until such time as a large number do so, the urban economy will be characterized by a high-income group and a poverty subclass of workers. Assume, finally, that local service industries (government and education) compete with the progressive industry for educated labor force, and must, therefore, pay a wage that increases at the same rate even though productivity in their local industries is not rising nearly so rapidly.

Given this set of not-unusual circumstances, one can show that the tax rate (on property, say) necessary to support the government budget for a fixed number of government employees depends on the relative size of the two export industries. The smaller the progressive industry relative to the stagnant industry and government employment, the higher the tax rate will have to be. The more rapidly the progressive industry wages grow the higher the tax rate and the more difficult it will be for the stagnant industry to remain in that area. In the extreme, the high-wage, high-technology industry serves to drive the low-wage stagnant industry from town, generates an unfavorable tax situation for any potential replacement industry, and, in the absence of replacement, leaves the low-wage employees totally unemployed.

Albin's model is allegorical, but it reflects a specific form of interaction between various aspects of the urban economy which is not unrealistic. Similar hypothetical modelling is needed for the relationships between, say, real wage levels in national market industries where nominal wages are determined nationally and increases in wage levels in local services that, when passed on in higher local prices, imply lower real wages for others. As our ability improves to characterize, model, simulate, and evaluate the economic processes that are present in urban economics, it is increasingly important that these distributional questions be addressed. Ultimately, to suggest today that average income levels are an appropriate measure of urban economic welfare is just as naive as it was twenty years ago to suggest that the level of economic welfare in any single United States city could be measured by national average income figures.

6

How Can the Development Prospects of an Area be Determined?

The principal conclusions of the preceding chapters may appear highly discouraging to the planner, public official, and concerned citizen. We have found that the economic development of any single city within the national system of cities is an immensely complex process, subject to substantial influence from outside the city. Local locational advantages depend on long-term changes in the location of population, the national composition of output, the allocation of government expenditures, changes in the age and skill composition of the local and national labor force, and changes in the technology that determines not only *what* we will produce and consume, but *how* and, therefore, *where* we shall produce and consume it.

Cities that seek to promote higher levels of local income cannot count on doing so simply by attempting to attract industries that are growing rapidly in terms of employment or output because there is no necessary connection between such growth and increases in income levels. Such cities cannot simply seek high-wage industries without careful analysis, for industries that have nationally high average wage levels may have substantial variations in wages over different areas in the country.

Cities that seek to stabilize employment levels or income levels are not likely to be able to do so efficiently merely by attempting to attract industries that appear stable nationally. And different patterns of expansion among existing industries may imply substantial differences in the implications for stability.

Reduction in local inequality in the distribution of income does not call for any simple, unambiguous policy choices in terms of industrial structure so far as is known to date. For cities in different circumstances, where "circumstances" include a myriad of characteristics ranging from the age, sex, race, and skill composition of both the employed and unemployed labor force to industry mix and rate and age composition of migration, the income distribution implications of identical policies will be different.

Furthermore, the overriding theme that has appeared with numerous variations throughout this book is the suggestion that the past, present, and expected future development of each city is likely to be more closely related to the individual locational history and present characteristics than to any common pattern of development among cities of comparable size or economic structure.

It may be that the most important question under such conditions would be a question asked with considerable anguish: "How, then, can we possibly learn what are the reasonable and feasible economic development alternatives open to our city or urban area?" In this chapter we review three major detailed studies of local area economic development in order to suggest some of the ways in which the question above has been approached and might be approached for any individual urban economy.

The three studies are (1) the New York Metropolitan Region Study, (2) the Economic Study of the Pittsburgh Region, and (3) the study by Stanislaw Czamanski of development potential for the province of Nova Scotia in Canada. The three studies differ in numerous ways. They were undertaken for three different (but overlapping) sets of purposes. They correspond to three very different regional economies. They have different formats and used different techniques to arrive at their conclusions.

But the three studies share characteristics that may make them important comparable examples of the kind of research necessary to determine, at the level of detail required by policy makers, the real nature and development potential of the respective local economies. They are all, for example, oriented to determining the nature of the locational advantages of the local economy in the context of national and international markets. They cover similar aspects of that advantage while using, and permitting comparison of, different techniques. They provide examples of attempts to define a local economy's unique economic and demographic characteristics and to relate them to past growth and development patterns. They also provide examples of three different scales of research projects, implying three different levels of cost and three different forms for organizing the study.

The New York Metropolitan Region Study was begun in 1956 at the request of the Regional Plan Association, a nonprofit research and planning agency for the twenty-two counties in New York, New Jersey, and Connecticut that comprise the greater New York metropolitan area. The study was conducted by the Graduate School of Public Administration of Harvard University over a three-year period under the general direction of Raymond Vernon. The entire research project resulted in the publication of nine volumes on various aspects of the economics, demographics, and politics of the region, plus a technical supplement (Berman, Chinitz, and Hoover 1960; Chinitz 1960; Handlin 1959; Helfgott, Gustafson, and Hund 1960; Hoover and Vernon 1960; Lichtenberg 1960; Robbins and Terleckyj 1960; Segal 1960; Vernon 1969). Vernon noted that the images evoked by New York range from those of "growth and vitality" to some of "decay and retrogression." The goal of the study was, he suggested, "to get behind these sometimes contradictory and always bewildering impressions and to identify the major forces which are at work in shaping the New York area's economic life" (1960, p. 1). Each of the component studies also attempted to project the characteristics with which it was concerned to the years 1965, 1975, and 1985. The study was more oriented to projections of that sort than to the organization of a program of coordinated regionwide policies for development.

The Economic Study of the Pittsburgh Region was undertaken from 1959 to 1962 by the Pittsburgh Regional Planning Association (PRPA) to assist those interested and engaged in the planning and development of the six-county Southwestern Pennsylvania region centered on Pittsburgh. It sought to provide "a groundwork of basic information and understanding of economic conditions in the region, and the factors affecting its development" and to respond to "an acutely felt need for detailed and objective diagnosis of the strengths and weaknesses of the regional economy" (The Pittsburgh Regional Planning Association 1963a, pp. v-vi). The study was organized under the directorship of Edgar M. Hoover and Benjamin Chinitz, employed some ten additional professionals at one point or another as consultants to the staff of PRPA, and resulted in the publication of three volumes (PRPA 1963a-1963c). Since the impetus for this study was more clearly related to local dissatisfaction with the slow population growth and economic growth of the region, its orientation and its analysis of alternative development possibilities corresponds more closely to the focus of this report.

The third study is not oriented to urban development per se, but it is focused directly on the problem of developing a set of economic development alternatives of a coherent regional economy. It also demonstrates the application of some advanced tools of regional science to the problem of area development. The study consists of a single volume, written by Stanislaw Czamanski (1972), in which the author unites the results of six three-month periods (summers) over 1966 to 1971 during which the author and several of his graduate students undertook research projects commissioned by unrelated agencies with respect to a single regional economy, the Province of Nova Scotia. The Czamanski volume focuses on the analysis of locational attractiveness and investment equilibrium as determinants of the growth of income, output, and employment in the region. It concludes by offering an econometric model of the growth process that is used to test the effects of alternative simulated development policies.

The New York study and the Pittsburgh study are considered to be among the most comprehensive ever undertaken. The Czamanski study represents, as we noted, application of some of the most advanced techniques. The fact that all three will manifest shortcomings may be considered evidence of the relatively primitive nature of the art or science of urban economics rather than evidence of inability on the part of their authors. All three studies, in fact, have incorporated some of the foremost experts in the field.

In order to provide a partial answer to the question posed at the outset of this chapter, we compare and contrast the techniques used in the three studies to analyze some of the principal locational characteristics of the local economy and to derive from them projections of the future economic structure and alternative development possibilities. We consider first how the economic structure of each area was described and how its special characteristics were determined. We look then at the determination of relative local labor market and transport cost characteristics. Finally, we compare and contrast the techniques used to forecast future economic structure and to derive development policy. The emphasis in this chapter, unlike that of previous chapters, will not be on the conclusions of the studies, conclusions most likely relevant solely to the areas studied. Our emphasis here will be on the techniques that were used to study the local economies.

Determining the Characteristics of the Current Economic Structure

The economic structure of a city has many dimensions that one could choose to emphasize. The three studies differed somewhat in both the dimensions that they emphasized and the measurement approaches that they utilized. The dimensions that are important depend, in part, upon the specific objectives that underlie any given study. The approaches or techniques used will depend upon the availability of data and the orientation of the staff producing the study.

In the New York study determination of the broad characteristics of the area's economy, especially manufacturing, was assigned to Robert M. Lichtenberg (1960). A separate study of the financial services provided in the region for local and national hinterlands was provided by Sidney M. Robbins and Nestor E. Terleckyj (1960). Lichtenberg's analysis (and to varying extents much of the analysis in other volumes of the study) was based principally upon a classification of 446 four-digit manufacturing industries into groups organized along dominant locational characteristics. This classification was developed in a relatively ad hoc fashion that is not described in detail anywhere in the study. In general, we are told, the locational orientation was "based on evaluation of clues suggested by a variety of sources: economic histories, economic geographies, published and unpublished industry studies, classifications published by others, and the locational patterns shown by the industries" (Lichtenberg 1960, p. 252). Industries were further divided within the transport-sensitive group into those that are pulled toward local or regional markets and all others.

Locally pulled industries were identified on the rather arbitrary basis of whether the proportion of national employment in such industries found in the New York Metropolitan area was no less than nine percent (the New York share of population) and no more than twelve percent (the New York share of personal income).

The categories developed were (a) inertia based; (b) transport-sensitive, local and regional; (c) transport-sensitive, national market; (d) labor-sensitive, skilled; (e) labor-sensitive, unskilled; and (f) external economy oriented. The last category proved to be the largest, but its definition appeared somewhat circular. *External economy industries* were identified as those with some or all of the following characteristics: (a) small, generally single-plant operations; (b) producing goods with frequent rapid changes in products; (c) generally unstandardized products, hence, few economies of scale; and (d) low ratios of inventories to sales. By virtue of the fact that many of the industries heavily concentrated in New York share such characteristics, and in the absence of other bases for location in the area, Lichtenberg assumed that the various forms of agglomeration economies thought to be available in the area must account for their presence.

A comparison of the distribution of total manufacturing employment among the various categories for the New York region and for the United States indicated that the area had only one-half the national average proportion of employment in transport-sensitive industries and only a little more than a third of the national market transport-sensitive proportion. On the other hand, external-economy industries constituted the largest single group, as noted above, and were present in New York at 2.5 times their national average share. From these facts Lichtenberg developed one of his two principal themes: that the New York region possessed a locational disadvantage for transport-sensitive industries and an obvious locational advantage for external-economy industries.

The second theme developed by Lichtenberg was that the region has been characterized by industries that nationally have grown more rapidly than average in terms of employment over the preceding twenty-five years, but that the region has not grown as rapidly as its component industries because competition with other regions of the nation had led to erosion of its share. On the other hand, he noted, the industries comprising the area economy had had slower than average growth in value added per employee (capacity to generate local income) that has accounted for the fact that expected growth in value added was below the national average.

Expected growth in both employment and value added were calculated from a shift-share standardization procedure similar to that which was discussed in Chapter 3. Expected growth rates were calculated primarily for national market industries in the regional economy and compared with actual growth rates experienced. From these comparisons Lichtenberg drew rough evidence of the extent to which the competitive shares and the industry-specific competitive position of the local economy were being weakened. From the difference between expected and actual employment increases for each of his major orientation groups, he was able to show, for example, that actual employment increases in labor-oriented industries in the New York region fell further below expected levels than external-economy industry increases, indicating further that New York may have retained a greater competitive advantage for the latter. Some variant of the same standardization and classification procedure was used in both of the other studies as well.

Given the preeminence of the New York region in terms of finance and insurance, a separate study was commissioned to determine the nature of that portion of the region's economy. This second study, by Sidney M. Robbins and Nester E. Terleckyj, sought to determine the locational characteristics of New York's leadership in marketing securities, commercial banking, insurance, and other financial services. The procedure consisted of viewing each of the individual industries separately, viewing the (generally declining) relationship between growth in the national economy and the share of each type of financial service provided by New York. Some regression analysis was used to relate employment in the banking sector to dollar investments, consumer loans, and other loans so that savings and credit projections could be converted to employment equivalents. Demand for New York financial services was divided into separate national and local markets, and the distinct determinants of each were analyzed. In this way it was possible to project that employment in the New York region in financial services would continue increasing absolutely while it continued to decline as a share of national financial employment.

Similar studies, though in less detail, are provided for several of New York's principal manufacturing industries in a third volume in the series by Roy B. Helfgott, W. Eric Gustafson, and James M. Hund (1960). The approach is similar: brief discussions of the growth and history of the industry relative to national and local growth, followed by analyses and interpretations of the future of the industry in the area. The most disappointing characteristic of the entire New York study becomes apparent when one tries to put together the results of all three studies. The coverage of economic areas is neither comprehensive nor well-integrated. Most nonmanufacturing activities other than financial services received only cursory treatment; the interaction between projections of manufacturing employment and, for example, employment in local financial services are not evaluated.

The Pittsburgh study appears to have been focused better and to have coordinated the contributions of its various staff members considerably more closely. The dimensions of the urban economy that were to be studied closely were determined by seven "facts of economic life" in the region: (1) slow population growth and net outmigration; (2) slow growth in employment; (3) low participation rates, especially for women; (4) ten years of unemployment rates above the national average; (5) per capita income rising slower than the national average; (6) a very mixed pattern of high and low wages; and (7) heavy concentration of employment in large manufacturing enterprises. The study then seeks to find the local determinants of these "peculiarities."

Comparison with nine other large cities establishes that the Pittsburgh region has a much larger employment per capita in primary industry (mining) and a low proportion of population in services. A Commerce Department study showed Pittsburgh to be less diversified than most of twenty major cities of comparable size. Calculation of *location quotients* (local per capita employment in an industry divided by national per capita employment) identified the detailed industry categories in which Pittsburgh was most specialized. Comparison of local employment per plant with national average indicated that local firms tended to be much larger than average.

In an attempt to explain the pattern, a survey of 460 plants was conducted to obtain information on employment levels, sources of materials, distribution of products, and attitudes toward locational characteristics of the region. The survey made clear that most of the output of the industries in which the economy was specialized was exported from the region, and the high proportion in mining industries could be explained by local abundance of coal and specialization in coke-fired iron smelting.

The fact that retail and service sales per capita are very low in the area was analyzed by means of multivariate analysis of various income levels, income distribution, and age distribution variables, with little success. Comparison of Pittsburgh labor force participation rates, proportion in blue-collar jobs, unemployment rates, and the distribution of income across different types of income with comparable data for the United States suggested that the higher than average demand for blue-collar workers, the lower-than-average demand for women, and the lower than average share of income from proprietors' income are closely related to the employment characteristics of the region's principal industries. But the chronic unemployment combined with higher than average income levels did not yield to such explanations. Answers were then sought in detailed analyses of the histories and production characteristics of the seven most important industry groups.

The individual studies lead to the conclusion that Pittsburgh, unlike New York, has tended to specialize in industries with unfavorable slow-growth characteristics. Early growth on the basis of heavy specialization in large-scale manufacturing during the late nineteenth century did not broaden into new industries and services. The large scale of operations in principal manufacturing plants, the study speculates, may have encouraged the development of many business services within the manufacturing firms and hindered the development of the independent service sector needed by incipient firms.

The Nova Scotia study provided both more comprehensive analysis of relative local development problems and more detailed statistical analysis of the economic structure of the region. Czamanski demonstrated, for example, that over the past fifteen years in Nova Scotia local per capita output (gross regional product) had hovered between sixty-two per cent and seventy-two percent of the national average; local wages and salaries averaged about seventy percent of the national level; and local business investment had been taking place at rates from ten percent to thirty percent below the national rate. Value added per capita in Nova Scotia was less than forty percent of the national average; the labor force participation rate (employees as percent of population) less than sixty percent of the national average.

The economic structure of the region, however, appeared to be the mirror image of the national structure. A slightly lower share in manufacturing and a higher share in government services were the principal distinctions. Czamanski quantified this similarity by means of comparative localization curves and indices of specialization (based on the ogive approach discussed in Chapter 4) for total employment. Czamanski attributed the failure of these measures to indicate sources of differences in welfare levels to the problems of working with industries at excessive levels of aggregation. The specific component industries found in Nova Scotia, he claimed, were characterized by atypical problems that would lead to misinterpretation if one assumed homogeneity. He then proceeded to analyze some of the specific characteristics of those industries that would tend to produce the incompatibility between national and local measures.

Czamanski also used shift-share analysis for total employment and for manufacturing and found that Nova Scotia had a small negative industry-mix effect (slow-growing industries, on average) and a highly negative competitive shift effect (loss of shares in markets). By looking then at the relationship between national growth and local growth on an industry-by-industry basis, he was able to identify those industries that were the strong points of the economy. The value of that approach was twofold: It provided a basis for evaluation of local industry growth rates (i.e., the national rate for that industry), and it permitted immediate identification of those industries for which the region was gaining advantage and those for which it was losing competitiveness.

The Nova Scotia study proceeded one step further in the analysis of the relative importance of individual industries and industrial sectors. Czamanski used an input-output table to organize all local production according to major category of final demand. That is, the input-output table permitted relating local production to the final consuming sector, whether consumption by individuals, consumption by federal and local government, new capital formation or exports. He found that government sectors accounted for as much as thirty-nine percent of income and thirty-eight percent of employment, while the export sector generated only twenty-two percent of incomes and twenty-four percent of employment. Without the use of the input-output table, it would not have been possible to assign proportions of employment in each industry to various final uses. Or, viewed from another perspective, estimates that do attempt to classify output by final use (including export-base models) are essentially guessing at the linkages for which the input-output table offers systematic estimates.

Determining Labor Market Characteristics

There are numerous dimensions of the local labor market that are potentially of interest in determining whether a concerted development effort is needed and what, if warranted, such an effort should consist of. If cities compete for employment and income, it is not sufficient to know local wage levels. One must also know wage levels in competing economies. To know relative wage levels at one point in time is not sufficient in a rapidly changing national or regional economy; it becomes essential to know how local wages have tended to move relative to tendencies elsewhere. The age and sex structure of the local population can be important determinants of average wage levels, for one would not expect an area with disproportionate shares of old or very young people to have average wages comparable to those of an area with large proportions in prime productivity ages. Differences in age and sex structure of wages and participation rates may indicate possibilities in which an area may improve its economic structure that are distinct from attempts simply to expand principal traditional industries.

Analysis of the labor market in the New York study was assigned to Martin Segal who prepared a complete and separate volume designed to generate "an understanding of the part that wage levels have played in conditioning the location of industries in the New York Metropolitan Region, and what part the wage factor may yet play in the future" (1960, p. 1). He approached the problem in four specific ways, after providing a general introduction to wages and skills as locational factors and to specific institutional characteristics of the region's labor market.

Segal's first step was to provide comparisons of various components of local wages with comparable statistics for other major urban areas. He was able to show that average weekly earnings over all employment in the New York area were less than the averages in five other metropolitan areas. In the manufacturing sector, they were lower than ten other areas, largely because New York manufacturing was specialized in low-wage industries. Detailed analysis, however, generated a conclusion precisely opposite to that which aggregate statistics would have suggested. For comparison of relative wage levels in those specific industries in other cities showed that wages in the New York region were higher than the levels in comparable industries in other areas with concentrations of those industries.

Segal then analyzed the trends in wages within the region relative to other major geographical areas, and in detail for seven large local industries (largely garment manufacturers) that his prior analyses had suggested were under wage pressures. Given the relatively high levels of New York area wages, he was particularly interested in learning whether the national trend toward convergence in wage levels would reduce competitive pressure on New York industries threatened by high local wages. He concluded that "these influences, though they may eventually result in a greater uniformity of wages throughout the country, do not necessarily produce a continuous and progressive narrowing of wage differentials in individual industries among urban areas and the rest of the country" (p. 91).

Segal attempted to analyze the local pressures on wage levels as a basis for predicting future trends and future wage-based problems. He described the interdependence of wage levels in various industries, especially the links between wage-sensitive industries and other local and national industries which were relatively insensitive to wage levels. He showed, for example, that office salaries in most categories were an almost constant proportion of salaries in the highest paid categories. General wage increases in the area and attributable largely to wage-insensitive industries were likely to decrease the attractiveness of the area for industries under wage pressure.

Finally, Segal pulled these trends together and recognized that the area was likely to lose wage-oriented industry but should be able to maintain and increase employment levels in those industries for which the region held other attractions. From this conclusion he was able to suggest development policy: Given the expectation of continued high wage levels, that which is needed is further strengthening of the region's skill levels by means of vocational training and rehabilitation programs.

Relative wage levels in the Pittsburgh area were determined on an even more detailed basis. From the various censuses of manufacturers and of business, data was gathered to provide a basis for comparing Pittsburgh wage levels in sixty-one separate manufacturing industry groups, thirty-two retail trade lines, twenty-five wholesale trade lines, and twenty-eight service lines found in Pittsburgh. For each, average hourly earnings (including all fringe benefits) were derived for Pittsburgh and expressed as a percent of the average across all of thirty SMSAs reporting employment in that category for both 1954 and 1958.

The Pittsburgh area was found to have an unusually wide spread in earnings levels, even among its largest industries. Above-average earnings appeared in industries with one or more of five characteristics: (1) heavily unionized, (2) large in the Pittsburgh area (on the basis of employment share), (3) preponderantly male-oriented, (4) high-wage nationally, and (5) more likely to have many employees per plant.

Trends in earnings were established over longer periods for manufacturing and construction sectors in the aggregate, and on a detailed basis. The trends were established by comparing increases in the Pittsburgh area with increases in each industry for the nation as a whole. Trends in local earnings indicated increases in excess of the national average that the authors of the study assert (but appear not to test) was attributable to the fact that a large share of Pittsburgh's employment was in industries that experienced a faster-than-average rise in earnings rates throughout the nation from 1949 to 1960. The study viewed those increases with mixed emotions, for although they clearly represented increases in the welfare of the workers receiving them, it was unclear whether they have been matched by productivity increases among local industries. The best indication they could find of the net effect upon employers was the responses in their survey to questions about the skill and efficiency of the labor force available to them.

The wage comparisons permitted the study to determine that "the aspect presented by the Pittsburgh labor market is in large measure determined by the eye of the beholder." More important, perhaps, it facilitated identification of the nature of the "beholders" most likely to find it appealing.

To a manufacturer or builder, the area's labor pool is likely to appear high-priced (per man-hour) in comparison with most other large metropolitan areas, and even more so in relation to the labor markets of smaller, non-metropolitan communities. The potential employer in non-manufacturing industries, on the other hand, finds wage rates in the area in many cases lower than those in other large metropolitan areas. . . . A businessman whose activity requires a large proportion of unionized male labor is likely to view Pittsburgh as a high-wage area; while one whose type of production and scale of operations are well suited to the employment of non-unionized women workers may well consider Pittsburgh's relatively low labor costs as an important competitive advantage [PRPA 1963a, pp. 110-11].

Czamanski analyzed labor force characteristics of Nova Scotia in terms of several dimensions in addition to wages. The detail with which he evaluated wage levels was less than that of the New York study or the Pittsburgh study. He showed that average hourly earnings of all hourly rated wage earners in Nova Scotia were lower than those of all other provinces by as much as thirty percent in 1966 and 1967. But he attempted no further analysis of the extent to which this was attributable to industry mix. He sought, however, to demonstrate the underutilization of the labor force. If the same proportion of the Nova Scotia labor force were employed as was characteristic of the nation, he found that local employment would have been 10.4 percent higher. Long periods of out-migration have left the area with an age-sex distribution of the labor force that differs substantially from that of the nation or from that of Ontario, the Province with highest per capita output and income levels. Czamanski standardized the Nova Scotia labor force in several ways to test labor force utilization rates. If the Nova Scotia population, for example, had the same age-sex distribution and the same participation rates, the labor force would be nearly twenty percent greater. Most of that difference, he found, was attributable to differences in participation rates; for if the Nova Scotia population had Ontario participation rates applied to its existing age-sex structure, the labor force would be nearly thirteen percent greater. Czamanski sees this as evidence of massive hidden unemployment and an important contributor to the low income levels of the area.

The Nova Scotia study also offers cursory analysis of seasonal unemployment. Czamanski calculated an index of seasonal unemployment based on deviations from a twelve-month moving average for unplaced job applicants. He found that unemployment varied from fifty percent to sixty percent above the yearly average during late winter months to forty percent below the average during early fall. The magnitude of partial unemployment was also established by determining the proportion of the labor force employed less than forty weeks a year.

Determining Characteristics of Local Transport Costs

There are at least three dimensions of the relationship between the local economy and local transport costs that are particularly worth knowing. First, one would like to know the extent to which local industry does actually ship, how far they ship, and what mode they use for both shipments of products and inbound supplies. To the extent that the hinter-lands defined by such distances are large, transport costs may play an im-portant role. Distance is relevant to transport costs only to the extent that actual rates are proportional to distance. In the United States the transport rate structure has evolved in a sometimes coherent, sometimes incompre-hensible manner. The result is a complex set of mode-specific transport rates that are not always intelligible in terms of distance travelled. One would presumably want to know the extent to which actual rates favor or disfavor an area economy. Finally, the transport rates are ultimately relevant only to the extent that they reflect costs of shipping to significant markets. Distances from an urban economy to a market must be weighted not only by the cost of transportation but also by the relative size of that market. Each of our three studies offers an approach to one of these sets of interests, but none attempted to cover all of them.

The analysis of the interrelationship between transport costs and the structure and growth of the New York regional economy was, again, as-signed to a single author who produced a separate volume. Benjamin Chinitz, the author of that volume (1960b), divided transport dimensions into two categories, those oriented to the Port of New York and those oriented to transporting local manufacturing supplies and products. Chinitz established that the port's "rise to dominance" was originally as-sociated with the concentration of United States population along the East Coast. The port also drew large quantities of immigrant labor that formed part of the basis for manufacturing growth. The area's share of United States foreign trade shipping had fallen consistently from 1921 to 1956, except for the years of the two world wars. He distinguished dif-ferent kinds of freight and showed that New York's competitive strength was still in the handling of general cargo, as distinct from standardized or bulk cargo.

Chinitz' approach to inland transportation is more relevant to our interests here. The study drew from Chinitz' own extensive experience in the analysis of transportation factors and from a special transportation survey sent by mail to 2,000 manufacturing plants in the area. The pur-pose of the survey was to determine the location of the area's principal manufacturing markets and its principal sources of supply. By asking each respondent to indicate what proportion of total shipments were generally sent to each of eight major areas, what modes of transport were used, and similar questions for inbound freight, Chinitz was able to determine, for example, that more than eighty percent of the region's shipments of manufactures to national markets in 1956 actually went to the region itself, to New England, or to the Middle Atlantic states. This was im-portant to the New York region; for Chinitz also demonstrated that transportation technology has reduced short-haul transport costs more than long-haul costs, leading to decentralization of industries previously engaged in concentrated production and long-haul shipping. The fact that the New York region's shipping is concentrated within, say, a 300 mile radius of the city was encouraging evidence that changes in transport costs would not reduce its competitive advantage as greatly as if its markets were more dispersed.

The Pittsburgh study also included a brief historical analysis of the water and rail transport advantages that gave Pittsburgh one component of its initial spurt of growth. The study then analyzed freight rates from Pittsburgh to principal market areas to the East and the West and compared them with some of its principal regional competitor cities (Buffalo, Cleveland, and Youngstown). Rate regulation was a major issue, for the study contended it is evident that "the historic pattern of rates within the East systematically denied to Pittsburgh its distance advantage over Buffalo. . . ." (PRPA 1963a, p. 194). But industry-specific analyses suggested that such rate deficiencies were not responsible for the relative or absolute declines in the region's basic industries.

A closer, though speculative, connection was seen between biases in rail rates and some products not produced in the region and between trucking rate biases and the scarcity of wholesaling and light manufactures. By comparing rates between Cleveland and points east, the authors demonstrated that trucking rates fail to preserve Pittsburgh's locational advantages. Disadvantageous truck freight rates were specifically given the blame for the fact that Cleveland appears to have two to three times as much employment per capita in wholesale distribution categories.

The Nova Scotia study included a somewhat more rigorous analysis of location as a function of distance and transport costs that yielded interesting statistical measures but lost the wealth of relevant details included in the other two studies. Czamanski calculated some generalized indices of accessibility for Nova Scotia to Canadian and United States markets. The indices are heavily transport-oriented, for they assume, among other things, that producers are solely interested in minimizing the costs of shipping, that transport costs are equal for all commodities and proportional to distance and weight, and that demand for all products is proportional to population, retail sales, or value added in manufacturing in each market. Three measures were calculated, one for each measure of market potential. Czamanski calculated such indices for each of the seven major ports in the Eastern Canada–Northeastern United States area. Halifax, the principal port of Sova Scotia was found to be in a position inferior to Toronto, New York, Montreal, Boston, and even Saint John, New Brunswick. Czamanski admitted that it would be easy to exaggerate the importance of these results. "The indexes derived are at best generalized indicators," he noted, "neither revealing the complex underlying relationships nor giving any clues to the future" (p. 13).

Projecting an Economic Structure for the Future and Deriving a Development Plan

The three studies considered here offer interesting comparison and contrast at this stage of the analysis also, for three different approaches were used for projecting economic structure and the other characteristics of the local economy on the basis of information garnered from the background studies.

A large proportion of the principal projections in the New York study were based upon Lichtenberg's shift-share analysis. To determine future industrial composition and overall employment levels (no attempt was made to project value added or wage levels), projections of national employment for eighteen broad manufacturing categories and ten non-manufacturing categories were developed and applied to derive projections of New York's increased employment by industry. On that basis alone strong continued growth was predicted for the region. But the region had been declining in its competitive share of most of its industries. For each major industry-orientation category used in the New York study, separate ad hoc projections were made of the rate at which the decline in competitive position would continue. For external-economy and labor-sensitive industries the projections called for approximate continuation of the 1929-54 trend. For other industries national processes of decentralization were assumed to mean that New York's share would move closer to its share of national population, thereby increasing, for example, its share of national market transport-sensitive industries. Application of these various assumptions on competitive shares to industry mix based growth estimates produced projections for 1965, 1975, and 1985 of employment by industry. Somewhat similar, but less systematic, bases were used by Robbins and Terleckyj to project employment in the financial sector.

Projections based on these techniques have two flaws embodied in them. The first is that they are no more valid then either the national employment projections with which one begins or the validity of the assumptions one has to make that competitive conditions will continue changing at approximately the same rate and in the same direction. Lichtenberg did not attempt to defend the national projections which he used, in spite of the fact that such projections have notoriety for their inexactitude. He did spend considerable time discussing likely trends in relative wage levels, transportation costs, and other determinants of the area's locational advantages and disadvantages.

Raymond Vernon, the study director, attempted to synthesize the first eight volumes in a closing volume that tended more toward forecasting than policy development (Vernon 1960). No specific recommendations for development planning were made; no major "problems" were identified. Rather, the study leaves one with the implicit conclusion that little public intervention in the region's economy is likely to affect either the rate or direction of its growth.

The Pittsburgh study, on the other hand, was organized around the recognition of common problems. Projections of its future were utilized to suggest the potential efficacy and the appropriateness of various policies. Projections and interpretation of background data were organized into one volume written largely by Edgar M. Hoover (PRPA 1963c).

The future economic structure of the region was estimated by means of an interindustry relations model that recognized not only the influence of national forces on individual industries (as in the Lichtenberg shift-share projects) but also the relations among industries within the region. The Pittsburgh economy was divided into twenty aggregate sectors of economic activity (major industry groups) and new survey data and prior survey information were used to determine the nature and the magnitude of sales by each sector to each other sector and, finally, to consumers, government, and to persons, plants, or institutions outside the region (exports). The table that resulted consisted essentially of an input-output matrix expressed in terms of employment rather than value of output.

Projections of export demand were derived from individual analysis of trends in each of the twenty sectors and incorporated in terms of separate high and low estimates. These demand projections were then adjusted for expected changes in output per employee and used to derive employment projections in the export sector. The export increases were then used, in conjunction with the local area employment input-output table to derive the indirect employment to be generated by increased exports.

Projections of employment related to the household (local-service) sector were derived, ultimately, from a disaggregated export-base multiplier that was assumed to remain constant over the entire projection period (1960 to 1985). This export-base multiplier was superior to the simplified multipliers criticized in Chapter 3 only in that there was a separate multiplier for each sector and that the aggregate multiplier was allowed to vary (as it should) according to the composition of exports.

The implications of the projections for the Pittsburgh economy appeared to be twofold. First, even if employment in the area should grow at the rates led by high export growth, employment increases would still require an average annual net out-migration of 8,800 persons to keep unemployment rates down. Low export growth and low unemployment rates would imply an average outflow of 28,900 persons a year; allowing the unemployment rate to remain at its 1960 level of 7.3 percent would reduce this flow to 17,800 per year, but would not eliminate it.

Second, substantial changes in the industrial structure and the resulting occupational distribution of the labor force appeared likely. Seven of the twenty industrial categories actually showed a decline; among manufacturing only metal products showed absolute and relative expected increases. Wholesale, retail, business, and personal services appeared to be the sectors of greatest expected growth. These employment changes would require reductions in the proportion of the labor force in the blue-collar categories and in unskilled labor. Increases were projected for proportions in professional and technical, managerial, clerical, and general service occupations. The overall implication, according to the study "should be clear":

> . . . the Region is going to have to adapt itself to sizable transitions over the next quarter-century. It must stand ready to shift people and physical resources from one activity to another, and to train and retrain individuals for changing and altogether new tasks . . . If even greater growth than that foreseen here were to be successfully accomplished, an even larger structural transition would be required [PRPA 1963c, p. 232].

The policy recommendations produced by the study reflect this theme of generating flexibility and adaptability to changes which are largely beyond the control of local planners. With respect to unemployment and out-migration, the authors of the study made a gentle and eloquent plea for continued out-migration as the lesser of two evils for both those who migrate and those who remain. While recognizing that out-migration may lower local morale due to "an anachronistic 'pioneer' tradition that population growth is the key to well-being—a notion long discredited in most other well-populated parts of the world" (p. 281), they suggested that the effects of chronic local unemployment are worse.

Among programs for action, they suggested: (a) attracting new industries such as metal-fabricating industries that would absorb local steel output; (b) improvements in labor-management relations so that the area would lessen its image as "strike-prone"; (c) raising the standard of basic education so that adaptation to problems and exploitation of opportunities would be increased; (d) raising the breadth and quality of technical and vocational training; and (e) establishment of more extensive retraining opportunities for older workers. Neither the likely impact of any of these programs, nor the relative effectiveness of one over the other were examined in the Pittsburgh study. The forecasting model that was formulated there did not permit such analysis.

The Nova Scotia study concluded wtih the formulation of a simple econometric forecasting model of the area economy that shared some characteristics of the New York and Pittsburgh approaches but that also incorporated a capability to simulate alternative policies and to choose among them, to a rough degree, in terms of their potential efficacy.

Czamanski combined numerous elements of his previous studies of individual dimensions of the Nova Scotia economy into a large simultaneous equation model that provided the opportunity to examine the quantitative and qualitative interrelationships of all the various dimensions. The model consisted of a set of fifty-four equations relating 104 characteristics of the local economy (predetermined variables, basic data variables, and intermediate variables) to eight target variables: total employment, total output, migration, educational levels, health levels, housing levels, and per capita income overall and in agriculture. It incorporated eight alternative policy instruments: government subsidies or investments in agriculture, manufacturing, housing and commercial services, direct government investment in transportation, education, etc., and other government payments or surpluses in the area.

The model was divided into seven submodels corresponding to (a) the iron and steel industry, (b) total employment, (c) total output and investment, (d) households, (e) government and exports, (f) population growth and migration, and (g) welfare. Simulation experiments were run on the model to test its sensitivity to changes in various variables, to test its ability to reproduce past conditions, and to forecast. Relationships between the target variables and the instrument variables, for example, appeared to be disappointingly small. Large increases (100 percent) in the various forms of government influence over the local economy tended to generate very small changes in, for example, per capita income or employment. Czamanski noted that such instrument variables had been at very low levels, "altogether insufficient for influencing the target variables. . . ." (1972, p. 331). Overall Czamanski found the levels of per capita income and employment in Nova Scotia most sensitive to new investment in its principal industry (iron and steel), value added in agriculture and mining, local wage and price levels, and taxes. These conclusions are not surprising for they represent the basic components of the models of regional income considered in Chapter 3.

Tests of the ability of the model to recreate past history in the area indicated that although it tended moderately to the high side (overestimating), "the vast majority of endogenous variables [those determined by the model itself] are estimated with an error under ten percent and most of them with an error less than five percent" (Czamanski 1972, p. 336). The model was then applied by the Nova Scotia Voluntary Planning Board to help in the formulation of a long-run development plan; some of their results, according to Czamanski, "shed light on the applicability and limitations inherent in aggregate econometric models, when used for regional planning" (p. 345). For example, an assumed 10 percent cutback in payments to military personnel (closing of a base?) were shown to cause declines in total local output by 2.6 percent, in employment by

1.9 percent, in housing investment by 13.6 percent, etc. Increases in government expenditures, distributed in varying amounts across different programs, were shown to yield little total change in total output but considerable increases in some dimensions of the quality of life.

Some of Czamanski's conclusions for the Nova Scotia economy, derived from the study, are instructive in themselves. He noted that policies oriented toward improved general infrastructure (roads, rail service, physical structures) have weak effects, "easily overshadowed" by other characteristics of industry analyses. For the organization of an industry-related development program, he noted:

> Not only do the existence, size, and character of previous industrial agglomerations constitute the major locational factor for many, especially small and medium sized plants, but one of the main obstacles to economic progress is the weakness of multiplier effects engendered by the small volume of interindustry flows within the province. Both considerations make it imperative to select carefully the type, size, and mix of industrial activities to be promoted with the help of limited public resources [p. 357].

Summary

It *is* possible to "get a handle on" the nature, the functioning, and the potential of urban and urban-area economies; but the task is not simple, and the loss in reliability associated with attempting to cut corners may be very great. There exists a wealth of data on the characteristics of cities, industries, and national development processes, the raw material of local development analysis. New models are emerging continually, as well as new techniques of analysis, new conceptualization of old problems, and new data sources.

The increasing quantification embodied in more recent modes of analysis reflects, on the one hand, improved tools for interrelating larger proportions of the full complexity of the urban economy. That quantification, on the other hand, may belie the imprecision of the tools, their limited usefulness, and the ultimate need that still remains to rely upon experienced interpretation of the results of the models in the formulation of urban development policy.

7 Research Needs in Urban Economic Development

We opened this book by asking a series of questions with respect to the goals that we tend to set for our urban economies. Some of those questions appear to have been answered relatively well by the literature reviewed. Many of them, however, remain cloudy or virtually unanswered. Let us first consider three overriding characteristics that future research on urban economic development should have if it is to provide better answers to those questions and answers that will prove as useful as possible to policy makers. Let us then raise a number of researchable questions about urban economic development processes that the existing body of research appears especially unable to answer and that development policy appears to require.

Basic Required Characteristics

Future research on urban processes would serve the needs of policy makers better if it possessed three focuses. First, the research should deal more explicitly with the developmental questions explored here rather than with aggregate growth questions exclusively. It is clear that one cannot model development processes without considering growth processes, but it is equally clear that the majority of urban and regional growth literature stops one crucial step short of becoming useful for development policy. There is little policy relevance to sheer growth, independent of its developmental implications. The implicit assumption that growth is synonymous with development is no longer tenable, either conceptually or politically.

Second, future research in the area should be even more explicitly policy relevant in the sense that it is cognizant of the present and likely future constraints placed on policy makers by political and institutional conditions. This is not to say that research that does not consider such constraints will not be valuable. Rather, there is a need for a level of research midway between those studies that merely analyze the phenomena of urban development and those that solely concern themselves with evaluation of past policy. There is a need for research on the interface between urban economic phenomena, urban development goals, and

109

the alternative instruments available to urban planners and policy makers. Research that bridges these levels of interest should be particularly encouraged.

Third, future research should recognize the information needs, information constraints, and information processing abilities of local area planning institutions. The development of techniques of urban and regional analysis that provide robust policy relevant data with a minimum of extra-local information requirements might be set as a target in this area. To the extent that conceptually attractive techniques of analysis require masses of data not readily available in local areas or from nationally gathered statistics, their policy relevance will be severely diminished.

Research needs: Analytical Techniques

There are numerous unresolved questions in the area of the basic determinants of the economic structures of urban economies that would, if answered, shed valuable light on the possibilities for urban development policies at the local level. Urban development policy might be facilitated more directly, however, by research directed toward new analytical techniques such as those suggested by the following questions.

How Can We Determine Better the Comparative
Advantages of the Local Economy?

The shift-share approach used most heavily in the studies reviewed here is several steps removed from actually identifying such characteristics. It fails to identify which dimension of an area's locational characteristics are responsible for positive or negative competitive effects. It frequently fails to distinguish between true competitive effects and pseudocompetitive effects attributable to excessive aggregation in the calculations. What is needed is, on one level, an analytical procedure by which one could match scientifically the production and distribution functions of all alternative industries with the input and market characteristics of individual areas to determine which industries are most likely to be able to function profitably in the local setting. Those who believe strongly in market allocation processes suggest that that is precisely the function performed by the market. Those who, like Harry W. Richardson, question the applicability or the efficiency of market allocation in the presence of spatial monopoly and economies of scale, suggest that such a procedure may be necessary. What we seek would be, in a sense, the local converse of interregional programming or industrial location models. For what is sought is not the most efficient allocation from a national perspective, but rather the most beneficial allocation from the local perspective. If this appears shortsighted, one must remember that the fundamental competition among urban areas for economic activity essentially calls upon each city to pursue its local interests, under the implicit assurance that the national goals of efficiency and equity will thus be served. What is needed is, on another level, a set of procedures for evaluating the long-term returns from investing local human and physical resources in specific industries and procedures for evaluating the effects upon those returns of alternative policies.

*How Can We Determine Better the Effects of Alternative
Rates and Patterns of Growth Upon Urban Levels
of Per Capita Income?*

If we can predict the employment composition, the likely levels and industry-specific rates of increase for wages, and direct and indirect effects on employment and output of specific projected economic growth, we need only cope with the migration responses to determine ultimate effects on per capita income. But to express the problem that way is to minimize the difficulty. For we have preliminary evidence from Richard F. Muth that migration and employment are simultaneously determined. What we need is an analytically and operationally simple model of the urban economy that permits estimation of the migration implications of alternative forms of economic growth or decline given local wage disparities and regional differences in propensity to migrate. What we also need is further research on the basic determinants of per capita income levels that eschews the questionable assumptions of both export-base and labor-supply approaches and that deals more directly with real spatial phenomena. The design of simulation models of the urban economy oriented to global development questions such as this and capable of being adapted to a wide variety of basic structures should also be a high priority. The emphasis, once again, must go beyond simulating aggregate growth and must extend to the estimation of average per capita and distributional implications of alternative rates and patterns of growth.

*How Can We Determine the Appropriate Weighting and
the Relative Significance of a Stability Goal?*

If the literature on stability suggests that development programs can be effectively oriented to increasing stabilization, it tells us little or nothing about the consequences of such an orientation with respect to alternative goals. To what extent will an orientation to stability imply policy inconsistent with increasing per capita income? If there is a trade-off, what relative weight should be given to the stability goal?

Other questions with respect to stability also remain unanswered. To what extent do the hypothesized high-wage implications of instability actually create wage differentials that run counter to regional competitiveness? What other benefits might be associated with stabilization or diversification policies? How might they be quantified? And How could diversification subsidies be designed so that the distribution of the cost of them corresponds to the incidence of the benefits?

How and to What Extent Can (and Should)
Distributional Questions be Introduced More
Explicitly into Urban Development Programs?

There is a vacuum of research in this area that has political implications. There is urgent need for models of urban development, on both the conceptual and theoretical plane and on the operational plane, that disaggregate the benefits of either unregulated growth and alternative planned growth across various socioeconomic classes and across different forms of income. Without such models it is virtually impossible to determine who benefits and how much, whether alternative distributional patterns would have deleterious implications for growth or stability of per capita income, or whether unregulated growth is even a source of inequitably distributed benefits. That alternative distributional patterns may occur is clear. Whether tacit acceptance of unregulated growth implies politically unacceptable distributional consequences cannot even be approximated without much further work in this area.

The fundamental nature of the research still needed in each of these areas, the urgency of it for informed and coherent policy making, and the breadth of the unresolved questions are all reflections of the underdeveloped state of the art. It is unlikely that such underdevelopment will be alleviated without encouragement to researchers to plunge into the conceptually complex field of policy relevant research. It is much more attractive in many ways to conduct research in the controlled laboratory conditions of abstract models than it is to attempt the same in the muddied, noisy battlefields of policy. The process of cumulative growth in policy oriented knowledge of urban development phenomena is not likely to thrive in the traditional laboratories unless preferentially cultivated. If it is to be encouraged, then this research review and synthesis may help to identify areas for priority encouragement.

References

Albin, Peter S. 1971. Unbalanced Growth and Intensification of the Urban Crisis. *Urban Studies,* 8, 139-46.

Alexandersson, Gunnar. 1956. *The Industrial Structure of American Cities.* Lincoln: The University of Nebraska Press.

Andrews, Richard B. 1953. Mechanics of the Urban Economic Base. *Land Economics,* 29.

————. 1956. Mechanics of the Urban Economic Base. *Land Economics,* 31.

Barloon, Marvin J. 1965. The Interrelationship of the Changing Structure of American Transportation and Changes in Industrial Location. *Land Economics,* 41, 169-79.

Berman, Barbara R.; Chinitz, Benjamin; and Hoover, Edgar M. 1960. *Projection of a Metropolis.* Cambridge: Harvard University Press.

Berry, Brian J. L. 1967. *Geography of Market Centers and Retail Distribution.* Englewood Cliffs: Prentice-Hall.

Bish, Robert L. and Kirk, Robert J. 1974. *Economic Principles and Urban Problems.* Englewood Cliffs: Prentice-Hall.

Borts, George H. 1961. Regional Cycles of Manufacturing Employment in the U.S., 1914-1953. New York: National Bureau of Economic Research Occasional Paper No. 75.

———— and Stein, Jerome L. 1964. *Economic Growth in a Free Market.* New York: Columbia University Press.

Bramhall, David F. 1969. An Introduction to Spatial General Equilibrium. In: *Locational Analysis for Manufacturing.* Gerald J. Karaska and David F. Bramhall, editors. Cambridge: The M.I.T. Press.

Brown, Douglas M. 1974. *Introduction to Urban Economics.* New York: Academic Press.

Chinitz, Benjamin. 1960a. The Effect of Transportation Forms On Regional Economic Growth. *Traffic Quarterly,* 14, 129-42.

————. 1960b. *Freight and the Metropolis: The Impact of America's Transport Revolutions on the New York Region.* Cambridge: Harvard University Press.

Christaller, Walter. 1966. *Central Places in Southern Germany,* translated by C. W. Baskin. Englewood Cliffs, N.J.: Prentice-Hall.

Clark, J. M. 1934. *Strategic Factors in Business Cycles.* New York: Harper and Row, 1934.

Clemente, Frank and Sturgis, Richard B. 1971. Population Size and Industrial Diversification. *Urban Studies,* 8, 65-68.

Conroy, Michael E. 1972. Optimal Regional Industrial Diversification: A Portfolio-Analytic Approach. Unpublished Ph.D. Dissertation, The University of Illinois at Urbana-Champaign.

————. 1974a. Alternative Strategies for Regional Industrial Diversification. *Journal of Regional Science,* 14: 1, 31-46.

————. 1974b. Spatial Equilibrium, Regional Industrial Diversification, and Rational Location Subsidies. Unpublished paper.

Crowley, Ronald W. 1973. Reflections and Further Evidence on Population Size and Industrial Diversification. *Urban Studies,* 10, 91-94.

Cutler, Addison T. and Hansz, James E. 1971. Sensitivity of Cities to Economic Fluctuations. *Growth and Change,* 2:1, 23-28.

Czamanski, Stanislaw. 1964. A Model of Urban Growth. Papers of the Regional Science Association, 13, 177-200.

————. 1972. *Regional Science Techniques in Practice: The Case of Nova Scotia.* Lexington: Lexington Books, D. C. Heath and Company.

De Vyver, Frank T. 1951. Labor Factors in the Industrial Development of the South. *Southern Economic Journal,* 18, 189-205.

Duncan, Beverly and Lieberson, Stanley. 1970. *Metropolis and Region in Transition.* Beverly Hills: Sage Publications.

Duncan, Otis Dudley and Reiss, Albert. 1956. *Social Characteristics of Urban and Rural Communities, 1950.* New York: John Wiley and Sons, Inc.

————; Scott, W. Richard; Lieberson, Stanley; Duncan, Beverly; and Winsborough, Hal H. 1960. *Metropolis and Region.* Baltimore: The Johns Hopkins Press, for Resources for the Future.

Florence, P. Sargent. 1948. *Investment, Location, and Size of Plant.* Cambridge: Oxford University Press.

Frech, H. E. III and Burns, L. S. 1971. Metropolitan Interpersonal Income Inequality: A Comment. *Land Economics,* 47, 104-8.

Fuchs, Victor R. 1967. Differentials in Hourly Earnings by Region and City Size. New York: National Bureau of Economic Research Occasional Paper No. 101.

Handlin, Oscar. 1959. *The Newcomers: Negroes and Puerto Ricans in a Changing Metropolis.* Cambridge: Harvard University Press.

Hanna, Frank A. 1954. Cyclical and Secular Changes in State Per Capita Incomes, 1929-50. *Review of Economics and Statistics,* 36, 320-30.

Heilbrun, James. 1973. *Urban Economics and Public Policy.* New York: St. Martin's Press.

Helfgott, Roy B.; Gustafson, W. Eric; and Hund, James M. 1960. *Made in New York.* Cambridge: Harvard University Press.

Hirsch, Werner Z. 1973. *Urban Economic Analysis.* New York: McGraw-Hill Book Company.

Hoover, Edgar M. and Vernon, Raymond. 1959. *Anatomy of a Metropolis: The Changing Distribution of People and Jobs Within the New York Metropolitan Region.* Cambridge: Harvard University Press.

Ilberis, Sven. 1964. The Functions of Danish Towns. *Geografisk Tidsskrift,* 63, 203-36.

Isard, Walter. 1956. *Location and Space-Economy.* Cambridge: The M.I.T. Press.

————. 1960. *Methods of Regional Analysis: An Introduction to Regional Science.* Cambridge: The M.I.T. Press.

Jacobs, Jane. 1969. *The Economy of Cities.* New York: Random House.

Knight, Richard Victor. 1973. *Employment Expansion and Metropolitan Trade.* New York: Praeger Publishers.

Kraft, Gerald; Meyer, John R.; and Valette, Jean-Paul. 1971. *The Role of Transportation in Regional Economic Development.* Lexington: Lexington Books, D. C. Heath and Company.

Kuznets, Simon. 1958. Quantitative Aspects of the Economic Growth of Nations, Part III. Industrial Distribution of Income and Labor Force by States, United States, 1919-1921 to 1955. *Economic Development and Cultural Change,* 6:4, Part 2.

Lampard, Eric E. 1955. The History of Cities in the Economically Advanced Areas. *Economic Development and Cultural Change,* 3.

————. 1968. The Evolving System of Cities in the United States. In: *Issues in Urban Economics.* Harvey S. Perloff and Lowdon Wingo, Jr., editors. Baltimore: The Johns Hopkins Press. pp. 81-138.

Latham, William R. 1973. Agglomerative Economics as a Factor in the Location of Manufacturing Industry. Unpublished Ph.D. Dissertation: The University of Illinois at Urbana-Champaign.

Lester, Richard A. 1945. Trends in Southern Wage Differentials since 1890. *Southern Economic Journal,* 11 (April).

————. 1946. Diversity in North-South Wage Differentials and in Wage Rates within the South. *Southern Economic Journal,* 12 (January).

————. 1947. Southern Wage Differentials: Developments, Analysis, and Implications. *Southern Economic Journal,* 13 (April).

Lichtenberg, Robert M. 1960. *One-Tenth of a Nation: National Forces in the Economic Growth of the New York Region.* Cambridge: Harvard University Press.

Lloyd, Peter E. and Dicken, Peter. 1972. *Location in Space: A Theoretical Approach to Economic Geography.* New York: Harper and Row.

Loesch, August. 1954. *The Economics of Location*. New Haven, Connecticut: Yale University Press.

McLaughlin, Glenn E. 1930. Industrial Diversification in American Cities. *Quarterly Journal of Economics,* 44, 131-49.

———— and Robock, Stefan. 1949. *Why Industry Moves South*. Washington: National Planning Association.

Madden, Carl H. 1956a. Some Spatial Aspects of Urban Growth in the United States. *Economic Development and Cultural Change,* 4, 371-86.

————. 1956b. On Some Indications of Stability in the Growth of Cities in the United States. *Economic Development and Cultural Change,* 4, 236-52.

————. 1958. Some Temporal Aspects of the Growth of Cities in the United States. *Economic Development and Cultural Change,* 6:2, 143-70.

Mattila, John M. and Thompson, Wilbur R. 1968. Toward an Econometric Model of Urban Economic Development. In: *Issues in Urban Economics*. Harvey S. Perloff and Lowdon Wingo, Jr., editors. Baltimore: The Johns Hopkins Press. pp. 63-78.

Morrissett, Irving. 1958. The Economic Structure of American Cities. *Papers and Proceedings of the Regional Science Association,* 4, 239-56.

Murray, Barbara B. 1969. Metropolitan Interpersonal Income Inequality. *Land Economics,* 45, 122-25.

Muth, Richard F. 1969. Differential Growth Among Large U.S. Cities. In: *Papers in Quantitative Economics*. J. Quirk and A. Zarley, editors. Lawrence: University of Kansas Press. pp. 311-55.

Neff, Phillip and Weifenbach, Annette. 1949. *Business Cycles in Selected Industrial Areas*. Berkeley: University of California Press.

Netzer, Dick. 1970. *Economics and Urban Problems*. New York: Basic Books.

Newhouse, Joseph P. 1971. A Simple Hypothesis of Income Distribution. *The Journal of Human Resources,* 6:1, 51-74.

Nourse, Hugh O. 1968. *Regional Economics: A Study in the Economic Structure, Stability, and Growth of Regions*. New York: McGraw-Hill Book Company.

Perloff, Harvey S. 1957. Interrelations of State Income and Industrial Structure. *The Review of Economics and Statistics,* 39:2, 162-72.

————; Dunn, Edgar S., Jr.; Lampard, Eric E.; and Muth, Richard F. 1960. *Regions, Resources, and Economic Growth*. Lincoln: The University of Nebraska Press.

Pfouts, Ralph W., editor. 1960. *The Techniques of Urban Economic Analysis*. West Trenton: Chandler-Davis.

The Pittsburgh Regional Planning Association. 1963a. *The Economic Study of the Pittsburgh Region, Volume 1: Region in Transition.* Pittsburgh: University of Pittsburgh Press.

————. 1963b. *Economic Study of the Pittsburgh Region, Volume 2: Portrait of a Region.* Pittsburgh: University of Pittsburgh Press.

————. 1963c. *Economic Study of the Pittsburgh Region, Volume 3: Region with a Future.* Pittsburgh: University of Pittsburgh Press.

Pratt, Richard T. 1968. An Appraisal of the Minimum Requirements Technique. *Economic Geography,* 44, 117-24.

Pred, Allan R. 1966. *The Spatial Dynamics of U.S. Urban-Industrial Growth, 1800-1914.* Cambridge: The M.I.T. Press.

Richardson, Harry W. 1969. *Regional Economics: Location Theory, Urban Structure, and Regional Change.* New York: Praeger Publishers.

————. 1973. *Regional Growth Theory.* New York: John Wiley and Sons.

Richter, Charles E. 1968. The Impact of Industrial Linkages on Geographic Association. Unpublished Ph.D. Dissertation, The University of Illinois at Urbana-Champaign.

————. 1969. The Impact of Industrial Linkages on Geographic Association. *Journal of Regional Science,* 9, 19-28.

Robbins, Sidney M. and Terleckyj, Nestor E. 1960. *Money Metropolis: A Locational Study of Financial Activities in the New York Region.* Cambridge: Harvard University Press.

Rodgers, A. 1957. Some Aspects of Industrial Diversification in the United States. *Economic Geography,* 33, 16-30.

Schreiber, Arthur F.; Gatons, Paul K.; and Clemmer, Richard B. 1971. *Economics of Urban Problems: An Introduction.* Boston: Houghton-Mifflin Company.

Segal, Martin. 1960. *Wages in the Metropolis: Their Influence on the Location of Industries in the New York Region.* Cambridge: Harvard University Press.

Siebert, Horst. 1969. *Regional Economic Growth: Theory and Policy.* Scranton: International Textbook Company.

Siegel, Richard A. 1966. Do Regional Business Cycles Exist? *Western Economic Journal,* 5, 44-57.

Stanback, Thomas M., Jr. and Knight, Richard V. 1970. *The Metropolitan Economy, The Process of Employment Expansion.* New York: Columbia University Press.

Steigenga, W. 1955. A Comparative Analysis and Classification of Netherlands Towns. *Tijdschrift voor Economische en Sociale Geografie,* 105-18.

Streit, M. E. 1969. Spatial Associations and Economic Linkages Between Industries. *Journal of Regional Science,* 9, 510-24.

Sufrin, S. C.; Swingard, A. W.; and Stephenson, Francis M. 1948. The North-South Wage Differential—A Different View. *Southern Economic Journal,* 15.

Thompson, Wilbur R. 1965. *A Preface to Urban Economics.* Baltimore: The Johns Hopkins Press, for Resources for the Future.

————. 1968. Internal and External Factors in the Development of Urban Economies. In: *Issues in Urban Economics.* Harvey S. Perloff and Lowdon Wingo, Jr., editor. Baltimore: The Johns Hopkins Press. pp. 413-62.

———— and Mattila, John M. 1959. *An Econometric Model of Postwar State Industrial Development.* Detroit: Wayne State University Press.

Tiebout, Charles M. 1956. The Urban Economic Base Reconsidered. *Land Economics,* 31.

————. 1962. The Community Economic Base Study. New York: Committee for Economic Development Supplementary Paper No. 16.

Tress, R. C. 1938. Unemployment and Diversification of Industry. *The Manchester School,* 9, 140-52.

Ullman, Edward L. and Dacey, Michael F. 1960. The Minimum Requirements Approach to the Urban Economic Base. *Papers and Proceedings of the Regional Science Association,* 6, 175-94.

————; Dacey, Michael F.; and Brodsky, Harold. 1969. *The Economic Base of American Cities.* Seattle: University of Washington. Center for Urban and Regional Research Monograph No. 1.

Vernon, Raymond. 1960. *Metropolis 1985: An Interpretation of the Findings of the New York Metropolitan Region Study.* Cambridge: Harvard University Press.

Vining, Rutledge. 1945. Regional Variation in Cyclical Fluctuations Viewed as a Frequency Distribution. *Econometrica,* 13, 183-213.

————. 1946. The Region as a Concept in Business-Cycle Analysis. *Econometrica,* 14, 201-18.

————. 1949. The Region as an Economic Entity and Certain Variations to be Observed in the Study of Systems of Regions. *Papers and Proceedings of the American Economic Association,* 39, 89-104.

Von Thünen, Johann Heinrich. 1826. *Der Isolierte Staat in Beziehung auf Landwirtschaft und Nationalökonomie.* Hamburg.

Weber, Alfred. 1929. *Theory of the Location of Industries,* translated and with an introduction by Carl J. Friedrich. Chicago: University of Chicago Press.

Wheat, Leonard F. 1973. *Regional Growth and Industrial Location, An Empirical Viewpoint*. Lexington: Lexington Books, D. C. Heath and Company.

Williams, Robert M. 1950. The Timing and Amplitude of Regional Business Cycles. *Papers and Proceedings of the Pacific Coast Economics Association, 4*, 47-51.

Wood, Robert C. 1961. *1400 Governments: The Political Economy of the New York Metropolitan Region*. Cambridge: Harvard University Press.

Index

Index

labor income, differences among
states, 56
labor market, 92; characteristics of,
97; distortions in, 66; larger and
more flexible, 28
labor market characteristics, 30
labor-oriented, 3, 20. *See also* industries
labor scarcity, 52
labor supply, 6, 111
labor-supply approach, 44, 48, 51
labor-supply models, 44; as presented
by Borts and Stein, 45
Lampard, Eric E., 4, 16, 31, 53, 55-
56, 59-61
large-scale wholesaling, 33
Latham, William R., 32
Lester, Richard A., 25
level of income, and the educational
level, 61
Lichtenberg, Robert M., 90, 92, 93,
103
Lichtenberg shift-share, 104
Lieberson, Stanley, and Duncan, Beverly, 4, 21-22, 68. *See also* Duncan,
Beverly; Scott, W. Richard; and
Winsborough, Hal H.
local consumption, 41
local cycles, 70
local market, growth of, 30
local money wages, increases in, 46
local requirements, 58
local sector, 42
local services, 43
local wages, comparisons of various
components, 98
location decision, 23
location factors: related to demand,
29; the relative importance, 29
location quotients, 95
locational advantage, 52, 89-90, 102
locational attractiveness, 91
locational characteristics, 49, 60, 68,
75, 92, 94-95, 110; dominant, 92
locational disadvantage, 93
locational influences, 67
locational orientation, 92

Loesch, August, 12
low income urban places, 61

McLaughlin, Glenn, 29, 72
Madden, Carl H., 16, 19
manufacturing, 5, 21-22, 33; "fabricating," 55; "raw-materials-oriented," 55; regional shift of, 24;
in sparsely populated areas, 29
manufacturing employment: growth
in, 31; increases in, 45, 53
market allocation, efficiency of, 110
market allocation processes, 110
market area, 13-14, 18, 21-22, 24, 73;
expansion of, 14; gradual erosion
of, 19
market area competition, 14
market attraction, 31
market orientation, 29-30
market potential, 23, 29
market power, 51
market size, 29, 31
markets, for products and factors of
production in each city, 10
markets for labor, disequilibrium in,
26
Matilla, John M., 30, 57, 61, 84. *See
also* Thompson, Wilbur R.
metropolis, 21, 37
metropolises: the nature of, 21; their
roles, 21
metropolitan employment, 58
metropolitan functions, 21
Meyer, John R., 24. *See also* Kraft,
Gerald; and Valette, Jean-Paul
mid-century bench mark, 21
migration, 15, 45-47, 52, 111; age-
selectivity of, 61; implications of
alternative forms of economic
growth, 111; indirect effects, 62;
potential effect upon per capita income, 62; rate and age composition
of, 89; within the United States,
62. *See also* out-migration of excess
labor
Milwaukee, Wisconsin, 21

minimum proportions, 35; of labor force in each industry, 33

minimum requirements, 34-35; increasing with city size, 34. *See also* economic structure

mobility of technical knowledge, 47

models of regional income, 106

monoply power, 50

Morrissett, Irving, 33-34 37

movement of capital, 47

Murray, Barbara B., 84

Muth, Richard F., 31, 44, 46-47, 53, 56, 59-61, 111. *See also* Dunn, Edgar S.; Lampard, Eric E.; and Perloff, Harvey S.

national goals of efficiency and equity, 111

national system of cities, 50

national variances and covariances, 74

national wage, a poor indicator of local wages, 57

natural resources, 23

Neff, Phillip, 70. *See also* Weifenbach, Annette

neoclassical approach, 48

neoclassical growth models, regional and urban variant, 44

neoclassical growth theory: background assumptions of, 48; full employment assumption, 48

neoclassical model, 48

neoclassical model of regional growth, 44. *See also* labor-supply approach

Netzer, Dick, 4

Newhouse, Joseph P., 84

New Orleans, Louisiana, 21

New York, New York, 95, 97-98, 101, 103

New York Metropolitan Region Study, 90

Nova Scotia, 91, 96, 100, 102, 105, 106

Nova Scotia Voluntary Planning Board, 106

Ontario, Canada, 100

orientation: to agglomerative linkages, 32; to labor costs, 32; to markets, 37; to raw materials, 29, 31-32

out-migration, as a policy, 105

out-migration of excess labor, 51

partial unemployment, 100

participation income, 41, 47

patents per capita, 20

patterns of trade among cities, 58

peak earnings, 40

per capita income, growth of, 57

per capita income levels, determinants of, 111

Perloff, Harvey S., 4, 31, 53, 55-56, 59-61, 74. *See also* Dunn, Edgar S.; Lampard, Eric E.; and Muth, Richard F.

personal income growth, 30

Pfouts, Ralph W., 42

Pittsburgh, Pennsylvania, 21, 95, 98, 102, 104-105

Pittsburgh Regional Planning Association, 91

population, and wage increases, 86; composition of, 1; size of, 1

population growth, 30; and the development of the urban economy, 63

population-sensitive industries, 86

potential output, 46; changes in, 47; determinants of, 47

potential reduction in expected unemployment, 80

Pratt, Richard T., 35

Pred, Allan R., 4, 16, 19

productive efficiency, 17

projected economic growth, effects on employment and output, 111

property income, 41

proportions of white-collar workers, 61

Providence, Rhode Island, 21

proximity to markets, 30

proximity to raw materials, 30

quality of life, 53, 81; improvement of, 17
quality of urban life, 63

raising urban income levels, hypotheses on, 51
ratio of capital to labor, 45, 57
raw materials, 29
real income, relative level of, 39
reallocation of capital and labor resources, 45
reducing instability, 78
regional development policy, 32
regional economic growth, composite model of, 46
regional growth, variation in, 32
regional hinterlands, 21
Regional Plan Association, 90
regional rivals, 15
regional social institutions, 46
regional stability, 71
regional transport system, 46
rehabilitation programs, 98
Reiss, Albert, 61, 68. *See also,* Duncan, Otis Dudley
relative income, 39
relative supplies of labor, 44
research: future, 5; policy related, 2
resource supply areas, 21
retail trade, 5
Richardson, Harry W., 48, 110
Richmond, Virginia, 21
Richter, Charles E., 32
Robbins, Sidney M., and Terleckyj, Nestor E., 90, 92, 94, 103
Robock, Stefan, 29
Rodgers, A., 72

St. Louis, Missouri, 21
San Francisco, California, 21
Scott, W. Richard, 21, 68. *See also* Duncan, Otis Dudley; Lieberson, Stanley; Duncan, Beverly; and Winsborough, Hal H.
seasonal fluctuations, 74; predictability of, 66

seasonal instability, 65, 68, 74; significance of, 65
seasonal unemployment, index of, 100
seasonally-complementary industries, 66
Segal, Martin, 90, 97
self-sufficiency of metropolitan areas, 59
self-sufficient farmers, 12
sensitivity to national cycles, 74
service employment, 33
service functions, 22
service industry, 13, 14; locational characteristics of, 33; as the principal source of new urban employment, 33
services: commercial and financial, 28; public, 28
shift-share, 93, 96, 110
shift-share technique, 59
Siebert, Horst, 44, 46-47, 85
Siegel, Richard A., 71
simulation models of the urban economy, beyond simulating aggregate growth, 111
size-distribution of cities, 18
small cities, 37
spatial agglomeration of industries, 32
spatial competition, among urban areas, 5
spatial concentration, 17
spatial monopoly, 110
specialization, 17
specialization of a city, 28
stability, 2; as an economic goal, 65; employment, 6; of income, 6; in the size distribution of cities, 19
stability goal: the appropriate weighting, 111; the relative significance of, 111
Stanback, Thomas M., 37, 54. *See also* Knight, Richard V.
Standard Industrial Classification, 69
standard of living, increases in, 1
standards of living for an urban economy, 46
state industrial development, 30

131

Steigenga, W., 72
Stein, Jerome L., 44-46, 48, 57. *See also* Borts, George H.
Stephenson, Frances M., 25. *See also* Sufrin, S. C.; and Swingard, A. W.
Streit, M. E., 32
Sturgis, Richard B., 76. *See also* Clemente, Frank
subsidies to diversifying industries, 79
substitute service centers, 18
Sufrin, S. C., 25. *See also* Swingard, A. W., and Stephenson, Francis M.
Swingard, A. W., 25. *See also* Sufrin, S. C.; and Stephenson, Francis M.
system of cities, 15, 18; competitive structure in the United States, 16; evolution of, 17

taxes on destabilizing industries, 79
technological change, 25, 45-46; labor-saving, 47
tendency to fluctuate, 73
Terleckyj, Nestor E., 90, 92, 103. *See also* Robbins, Sidney M.
terminal facilities, 28
terms of trade, changes in, 47
theorems on differential growth, 44
theoretical instability, 79
theories, construction of, 4; testing of, 4
Thompson, Wilbur R., 4-5, 30, 50-52, 57, 61, 65-66, 68-69, 74, 79, 82-85. *See also* Matilla, John M.
threshold effects, 20
threshold sizes, 20
Tiebout, Charles M., 41
Toledo, Ohio, 21
total employment, increases in, 42, 46
traffic flows, 66
training, of low wage workers, 25
transfer economies, 27
transfer payments, 41
transport advantages, 102
transport costs, 28, 48, 92; and competitive advantage, 102; determining characteristics of, 100; of finished products, 29; and the local

economy, 100; mode-specific, 101; of raw materials, 29
transport inputs, 23
transport modes, 25
transport-oriented, 23
transportation costs, 23-24, 30; changing, 24; the decreasing share of, 25; reduction in, 24. *See also* costs of shipping, 23
transportation systems, locational attraction of, 25
Tress, R. C., 72

Ullman, Edward L., 33, 35. *See also* Dacey, Michael F., and Brodsky, Harold
unionization, 31
unregulated growth, 112
unstandardized goods, 28
urban affluence, the determinants of, 40
urban area analysis, 55
urban conflict, 6
urban development, 46, 91; hypotheses specific to, 47
urban development policy, 6; dynamic nature of, 11; formulation of, 107; obstacle to the formulation of, 48; possibilities for, 110; proper objects of, 40; unrealistic goals, 40
urban development programs, 39; for whom, 86; objectives of, 86; oriented to diversification, 75; the organization of, 57
urban economic development, 1; characteristics of future research, 109; distribution of benefits, 81
urban economic structure, 51
urban economics, primitive nature of, 91
urban economy, 9; the basic determinants, 9; as a general equilibrium phenomenon, 10; overriding general characteristics, 9; strengths and weaknesses of, 6
urban employment, industrial composition of, 50

urban growth, 1, 19-20, 41; advocates of, 1; model of, 46; United States, 18
urban growth processes, 53
urban hierarchy, 16, 18, 22
urban income levels, 58
urban industrial diversity, 73
urban-industrial growth, 20
urban instability, three kinds of, 65
urban life, quality of, 1
urban population growth, 53
urban public infrastructure, inefficiently utilized, 66
urban residents, welfare of, 53
urban system, 5, 20
urbanization: and development, 17; rate of, 17
urbanization economies, 28. *See also* economies of scale external to an industry
urbanization tendencies, in the more-developed countries, 17

Valette, Jean-Paul, 24. *See also* Kraft, Gerald; and Meyer, John R.
value-added, distribution of, 5
value-added per employee, 58
value-judgments, 1
variances, 74

Vernon, Raymond, 28, 90, 103. *See also* Hoover, Edgar M.
Vining, Rutledge, 67, 71
vocational training, 98
Von Thünen, Johann Heinrich, 11

wage differentials, 25
wage increases, and productivity increases, 99
wage levels: attributable to industry mix, 100; interdependence of, 98; the local pressures on, 98; and underutilization of the labor force, 100
wage rate, 46
wages, industry-specific rates of increase, 111
Weber, Alfred, 11
Weifenbach, Annette, 70. *See also* Neff, Phillip
welfare, measure of, 6
welfare increases, without population increases, 31
Wheat, Leonard F., 31-32
Williams, Robert M., 70
Winsborough, Hal H., 21, 68. *See also* Lieberson, Stanley; Duncan, Beverly; Scott, W. Richard

Youngstown, Ohio, 102

About the Author

Michael E. Conroy received the B.A. in Economics and Latin American Studies from Tulane University in 1968, the M.S. in Economics in 1971 and the Ph.D. in Economics in 1972 from the University of Illinois at Urbana-Champaign. He is currently Assistant Professor of Economics at the University of Texas at Austin. Professor Conroy teaches and conducts research in the areas of Regional and Urban Economics, Population Economics, and Latin American Economics. He has published articles on these topics in the *Southern Economic Journal,* the *Journal of Regional Science, Land Economics,* and the *Latin American Research Review.*